Fenton Glass
The First Twenty-five Years
1907-1932

by william heacock

Featuring the glass collection on display at
The Fenton Art Glass Museum
Williamstown, W.Va.

Photography by
RICHARDSON PRINTING CORP.
Marietta, Ohio 45750

DEDICATION

To the memory of
Frank L. Fenton
(1880-1948)

Published and Distributed by:

O-VAL ADVERTISING CORP.
P.O. Box 663
Marietta, Ohio 45750

TABLE OF CONTENTS

FOREWORD

This book was a definite challenge to me. My research for the past seven years had been limited almost exclusively to pattern glass of the Victorian era. The Fentons started producing glassware at Williamstown as this era was gradually coming to an end, and styles and colors in glass production were beginning to change. When Mr. Fenton approached me about publishing this book, I must admit a great deal of hesitancy concerning writing a book about an era of glass production with which I was unfamiliar.

However, as I browsed through the newly opened Fenton Glass Museum, and as I studied the many original catalogues from the company's early years, I realized how important this book was. In adjusting my lack of knowledge, I read every book available on the subject of carnival and stretch glass. The tremendous void of data concerning early Fenton was obvious, so I forged ahead into an encounter with a later era of glass production.

I also was aware of the fact that it would be the glass, not the author, which would be telling it's story. With the modern photographic and printing technology available today, I wouldn't need to bore readers with long, wordy descriptions of pattern intricacies. The camera would also be able to capture the iridescent highlights which are unrealized by words and sketches.

The decision was also made to let the catalogues tell their own particular story. Most are reprinted in this book at considerable expense in their original color. Before I started my career in glass research, I often wished that earlier writers had shared more of their personal files with readers. I am certain there is a bit of "arm-chair" researcher in all of us. Many times I have leafed through the ad reprints at the back of the Kamm pattern glass books and found data which she inadvertently, but quite understandably, overlooked. I even receive letters from readers of my own books, pointing out facts brought to light from my ad reprints about which I was unaware. Frank Fenton is to be highly commended for his permission to share these priceless catalogues with readers of this book.

Perhaps some readers will be disappointed by the 1932 cut-off date. With 72 pages of color, we had to draw the line somewhere. I believe that the glass made during the second 25 years of this company should be covered by a separate publication, so plans for this sequel are being discussed. The ever-popular Fenton Hobnail was introduced during this later era, beginning in 1939. With patience and favorable reader response, perhaps it won't be long before this sequel is published.

ACKNOWLEDGMENTS

This book would not have been possible without the efforts of Frank M. Fenton, who contacted me in 1975, expressing an interest in obtaining my services as author of a book on the early production of the Fenton Art Glass Company. He flattered me by writing that "many have asked (permission) to do this and we have always resisted. Your books show me that it can be done well." I replied that I was honored by his request, but could not possibly fit it into my schedule until 1977. We began work on this book the summer of that year. Mr. Fenton was never too busy to offer help or advise during the strenuous photography sessions. He provided me with all the publications and catalogues I could possibly need. Production on the book lasted months longer than expected, and Frank never once complained about the inconveniences brought on by constant delays. There are just not enough words to properly express my appreciation to this outstanding individual, a man whose fervent interest in early American glass led to the opening of a superb glass museum and the publication of this book.

I also want to thank Bill Fenton for his efforts in making our photography sessions at the museum much simpler. And I will never forget the unselfish and endless help provided by Mrs. Helen Warner.

A special word of praise should be extended here to Dr. Eugene Converse Murdock, who in 1968 underwent thorough research concerning the early history of the Fenton Art Glass Company. Most of the historical information presented in this book came from his efforts. I also must thank Dr. James Measell, noted authority on Greentown glass, for sharing information concerning Fenton's early years, much of which was used to update the Murdock history.

For loans of glass pictured in this book, I must again thank Frank Fenton and the staff and personnel of the Fenton Glass Museum. This superior museum includes not only glass by Fenton, but also glass made in the Ohio River Valley, from Williamstown to Wheeling. Naturally the emphasis is on locally produced Fenton glass, but the displays of Northwood, Millersburg, Imperial and Riverside glass, among others, are most impressive. The glass illustrated in this book is only a fraction of that on display.

I also want to express my deepest appreciation to Bill Crowl, James Measell, Jim Broom, Fred Bickeheuser, Bill Carroll, Bob & Jean Brocke, Jack Burk, and Mr. & Mrs. Robert Hefner. All of these dear friends loaned me glass or information for this book, and I consider it a real pleasure to have known them. A special thank you to Mrs. Jean Cline for lending me several unusual rarities shown.

A final word of thanks to three wonderful friends who were with me all the way on this book; Bobbi Kuenz, my secretary, who helped me write and edit this book, Dave Richardson, who is directly responsible for getting this book done in the first place, and the photographer, Dale Brown, whose brilliant work you are now holding in your hands. God bless you—I couldn't have done it without you.

The Fenton Art Glass Company

A HISTORY OF THE FIRST TWENTY-FIVE YEARS

Researched and Written By
DR. EUGENE C. MURDOCK
Professor of History, Marietta College

Editor's Notes by
WILLIAM HEACOCK

Earliest known photograph of "newly constructed" Fenton factory—a picture postcard dated January 31, 1907.

INTRODUCTION
by
William Heacock

In honor of Dr. Murdock and the years of research invested in his history of the Fenton Art Glass Company, I have chosen to reprint here his own introduction to his 194-page typed manuscript. For readers of this book who are primarily interested in the company and not the glass itself, you are in for a special treat, because Eugene Murdock has done a magnificent job. Our original intention was only to offer readers a brief outline of events in the company's history, and concentrate primarily on the mountainous glass production of the first 25 years. However, after reading Dr. Murdock's history, I felt, with the concurrance of Frank Fenton and my publisher, that we could use much of his original words in context.

However, I have edited some of the history because of space limitations and to conform with the time frame of the title. I have also included data which has become available since 1968. When a sequel to this book is printed we expect to include the later years of Dr. Murdock's history.

FOREWORD
by
Dr. Eugene C. Murdock

This history of the Fenton Art Glass Company had its origins in the First Methodist Church in Williamstown, West Virginia, one Sunday morning in August 1964. On our way out of the sanctuary following the service, Frank M. Fenton inquired if I would be interested in attempting to write such a history. It took but a moment's thought to conclude that I would like very much to tackle the job. Personal curiosity was certainly one impelling motive, but more than that was the conviction that here was an important story which needed telling, and the sooner the better.

Work began almost at once and continued for about three years and four months. In the course of my research and writing of the history a number of people inquired "when will it be finished" and "what is taking you so long?" I frankly had hoped it would be completed sooner, but other matters kept getting in the way, so there were long periods when I had to put the work aside. Of course, I did not forget about it, and I would turn back to it at every opportunity, but still the long delays were unavoidable. It might also be pointed out that the deeper I got into the subject, more and more material began to appear, and in consequence of this the history became more detailed than was originally planned. On and off, since my first interview with Frank M. Fenton on August 18, 1964, until the writing of this preface on December 17, 1967, I have spent over 650 hours on this history.

As far as source materials are concerned, I should say that I have been given free access to all Fenton Company records up to 1950, which by mutual agreement was fixed as a cutoff date. Financial information after that date could not be used because of its possible adverse effect upon recent and current business operation, and this restriction was acceptable to me. Other than that there were no prohibitions. All documents I asked to see were given to me, and many more that had been mislaid and not looked at in years were found and turned over to me. In the *use* of the material I had free access to, in writing the history, reasonable and commonsense restrictions were in force. These applied to financial statistics of a privileged character. The absence of these statistics in no way detracts from the company's financial picture, as it is presented in the text. Even if such absence did tend to distort the picture, the substance of the material is actually used in paraphrase form.

I should like to say that this labor of some 1217 days has been intensely interesting to me and has brought me great satisfaction. I have gotten to know many people—old and young—whom I would never otherwise have met. A number of persons I knew I now know better. I have learned much about the town of Williamstown which I was not aware of. What gives me the most satisfaction, however, is the knowledge that there now is a history of the Fenton Art Glass Company. It is unlikely that this history will prompt massive revisions in our interpretation of American history, but it certainly will add to our understanding of local history, and from the business standpoint, it will enhance our understanding of the hand glass industry.

Frank M. Fenton, president of the Fenton Art Glass Company, who back in August 1964 asked if I would be interested in undertaking this job, has naturally been of tremendous help. I like to think that this project became a kind of hobby with him, one that perhaps he is sad to see completed. The countless hours we spent discussing the company's history with one another and with many others, were like voyages of exploration into uncharted seas. We never knew what fresh bit of information might spring forth; maybe something we had not heard about, or possibly some conflicting slant on a subject we thought was closed. It was an experience of continuing anticipation and excitement. We did not know too much, especially about the early years, when we started in, but as the work progressed, and as the material mounted, we filled in most of the gaps.

I have devoted so many hours to this work that my subject—as is the case with most historians—has become a part of my life. I know the Fenton family better than I know my own. And, again, it has been a rewarding work—giving both pleasure and satisfaction—and I am happy now to turn it over to the reader, trusting that he will excuse the long delay, and find it a story worth reading.

Eugene C. Murdock

Williamstown, West Virginia
December, 1967

I
HOW IT ALL BEGAN

It is unlikely that many of the Founding Fathers of the Fenton Art Glass Company (FAGCO) would have been willing to predict a long and prosperous career for their infant enterprise at the time it was organized in April, 1905. While they certainly hoped for many years of success and prosperity, they were thoroughly familiar with the countless hazards, natural and supernatural, which beset small hand-operated glass factories. Many such companies, for example, succumbed to fire, which would frequently begin in their hot metal works and envelop the wooden frame structures before any warning could be sounded. Others, which did well financially in their early years, would find it impossible to continue once their founder died. And still others, not plagued with fire or death, were simply unable to compete with better-financed rivals when automation and foreign competition entered the picture. The "Glass Works Graveyard" is filled with corpses of companies which flourished in the "golden age" of 1895-1910, but later fell victim to these forces.

Recognizing the risks involved, the Fenton people must have been somewhat apprehensive of the future as they entered the business world, but they were young, intelligent, and hard-working men, and they were not going to permit those risks to deter them. And not only did they survive while most of their competitors fell to the side, but their company would become one of the leading manufacturers of hand-made art glass in the country, selling its goods throughout the entire world. While the Fenton story is not necessarily fashioned in the Horatio Alger mold, it is a success story which has its moments of failure and despair. It is an interesting story and an exciting one.

The central figure in this narrative is Frank Leslie Fenton, born in 1880 in Indiana, Pennsylvania, the youngest of seven children, six of them brothers. He graduated from high school there on May 1, 1897, being chosen class valedictorian. He contemplated a teaching career for a brief period, as the files contain a letter of recommendation in his behalf to the school board of a nearby district. The letter said that he had "the qualifications and elements about him that go to make up a successful teacher if he was given an opportunity." Young Frank, however, never followed through on this, preferring to cast his future in the glass-making industry. He was apprenticed at the Indiana Glass Company in his home town the very year of his graduation, and became a foreman in 1898.[1] In 1900 he went to work at the Jefferson Glass Company just then opening its doors in Steubenville, Ohio.[2] Later he was employed at the Bastow Glass Company at Coudersport, Pennsylvania. When fire destroyed the latter plant, Frank moved to Wheeling and got a job at the Northwood Glass Company. "My particular work was in the matter of design," he recalled, "and then I got the idea that if I could do this work for an employer, I certainly could do something for myself."

[1] Harry Northwood was running this factory at this time, and the name of the company was changed two years before. However, the town residents, even to this very day, often refer to their local factory as the Indiana Glass Company, perhaps because it honored the name of their town.

[2] It is interesting to note that Harry Bastow was president and general manager of the Jefferson factory at this time. Thus, the strong similarities in glass made by Northwood, Jefferson, Fenton

and Coudersport can be somewhat understood. Bastow established his Bastow Glass Company at Coudersport in late 1903. In May of 1904, a local paper advertised seeking 25 girls to work in the plant's decorating department. Job seekers were to report to "F. L. Fenton, Manager Decorating Department." However, that month the factory was virtually destroyed by fire, and was never re-opened. The company's assets were used to pay labor claims — among them, $18.00 to John W. Fenton and $69.22 to Frank L. Fenton.

ROBERT C. FENTON
(1868-1948)

FRANK L. FENTON
(1880-1948)

JOHN W. FENTON
(1869-1934)

On May 4, 1905, Frank L. Fenton deposited in the Dollar Bank in Wheeling $284.86, which has given rise to a romantic legend about the company's humble origins. As it was handed down in the family circles, John once told Frank that if the latter ever wanted to go into business for himself he should call on John for financial help. Frank called on John and was asked, "How much money do you have?"

"$284," was the reply.

"Good," remarked John. "Between the two of us we now have $284.86. Let's get started." Although additional funds were needed before work could commence, and these would be raised by stock sales, this original amount probably took care of some of the petty initial costs.

Throughout the summer of 1905 a few other modest sums were also banked, but it seems evident that the company had little income in those early months. From May 4 until September 9 only $997.87 went into the company's account. However, on September 21 $300 was deposited and by January 20, 1906 nearly $5,000 more was banked. This sudden affluence suggests two developments: first, the company was moving into full-scale production by late September; second, stock sales were progressing satisfactorily, further fattening up the treasury. Page nine of the *PayRoll Record Book* (1905-07) lists the total cash received from early stockholders as $6,125.

So it was that in July 1905, Frank and John opened up their own decorating shop, the Fenton Art Glass Company, in Martins Ferry, Ohio. Having built a kiln in a rented, abandoned factory[3], they began purchasing "blanks" from different glass companies, cutting their own design on the blanks, and selling them. Another brother, Charles H., who had been employed at the Northwood plant, soon joined his brothers with the decorating company. Although the Fenton brothers were prime movers in the organization, two of the company's original officers were not Fentons. The President was J. C. Dent, a Bridgeport, Ohio druggist, and the treasurer was Dr. J. O. Howells, a medical doctor also from Bridgeport. John Fenton was vice-president, while Frank was secretary and general manager. Charles held no official post at first, other than "Head of the Decorating Department."

The first Board of Directors consisted of John and Frank L. Fenton, Dent, Howells, and G. W. Crook. In November, 1906, on the eve of the company's move from Martins Ferry to Williamstown, West Virginia, Charles H. Fenton supplanted Crook on the Board. A year later, after the company had become established in the Marietta suburb, a new slate of officers was chosen: John moved up to the presidency, Frank retained his posts as secretary and general manager, while adding that of treasurer, and Charles replaced John as vice-president. Apparently Dent and Howells felt it was too impractical and inconvenient to remain officers in a company which was located some 80 miles away. So while resigning their official positions they remained members of the Board of Directors and would ride the Baltimore and Ohio train down to Williamstown once a month for board meetings, and re-

turn home in the late afternoon. Dent was still on the board at the time of his death in 1924, while Howells resigned his post in 1942.

An intriguing, yet unclear chapter in the Fenton story deals with the circumstances attending the move to Williamstown. The questions which occur are two: (1) Why did the Fentons decide to abandon mere "decorating" and jump fully into glass manufacturing? and (2) once the decision was made to build a glass factory, why was Williamstown selected? The first question may be quickly answered. Many of the glass companies, from which Fentons bought their "blanks," also did their own decorating, hence they were creating a competitor in selling to Fenton. At first they perhaps reasoned that since FAGCO might not last long, it would not hurt to sell to it. However, as the new decorating company began to prosper, the glass companies gradually cut back their blank shipments until Fentons had nothing to decorate. Thus to obtain glass articles it became necessary for FAGCO to build its own glass plant. This decision was probably reached sometime in the spring of 1906

However, the other problem of "why Williamstown?" is not so readily resolved. Although the general account seems clear enough, there are a number of little details which require clearing up and a number of diverse stories which do not dovetail very neatly. An important person in this phase of Fenton history is Harry Bastow. Bastow was a veteran glassworker, with considerable experience in managing glass plants. Frank Fenton met him when working at the Indiana Glass Company, and became attached to him. It was said that whenever Bastow moved to a new glass plant, he took young Frank with him. Bastow, as manager, wanted Fenton to handle the decorating end of the business, and they operated in three or four different factories in this fashion.

Early in 1906, while working in Pittsburgh, Bastow decided to join the Haskins Glass Company in Wheeling as general manager. In June of that year, however, he quit Haskins and went with Fentons in an unusual capacity. Fentons by now had decided to enter the glass-making business themselves, and they no doubt reasoned that a man with Bastow's experience would prove helpful to them in getting started. No written contract was signed between FAGCO and Bastow, a fact which would prove embarrassing later on, but it was agreed orally that Bastow should visit a number of locations and recommend to the company the most suitable place to build its new factory. Once the site was determined, Bastow would then draw up the specifications for the building, order supplies, hire a work force, and supervise construction of the factory. A number of other miscellaneous functions were also assigned him, such as engaging an agent in New York City, and ordering equipment, like molds and pots, for the new structure. Then when construction was completed and production ready to commence, Bastow would become factory manager of the plant, a post he had held for many other companies.

In spite of this elaborate oral contract, there is little evidence to show that Bastow had much to do with the move to Williamstown, although, admittedly, the details are very incomplete. Along with other Fenton people, he did make three trips to Shadyside,

[3]*The factory which they occupied was the old West Virginia Glass Company, makers of Medallion Sprig, Scroll with Cane Band, and I.O.U. patterns.*

Ohio, where the prospects seemed fairly bright for purchasing an existing plant. He also made one trip to Barnesville, Ohio, and eight to Williamstown. However, at this point, another mysterious figure enters the scene, one who appears to have been more instrumental than Bastow in bringing the town of Williamstown and the FAGCO together. I. H. Terrell, 35, was an experienced glass man, living in Bellaire, Ohio. He had worked in various factories for twenty years from carrying-in boy all the way up to plant manager. In some fashion the citizens of Shadyside engaged Terrell to secure a glass company for their town to replace the Leighton Glass Company, which was on the verge of either moving or closing down.

Terrell inquired about the matter in the Wheeling area and was directed to John Fenton by George Hipkins of the Hipkins Novelty Mold Shop, a neighbor of FAGCO's in Martins Ferry. As a consequence, sometime in May, 1906 John and Frank Fenton, Hipkins, and Bastow went to Shadyside, where they met Terrell and officials of the company, and were given a guided tour. On the second Shadyside excursion, a week or so later, the Fenton people conferred with a number of citizens about the prospects of moving there. Bastow made one more trip to Shadyside, presumably by himself, a short time after that.

The efforts of Terrell, the citizens of Shadyside, and the Fenton people to locate FAGCO in Shadyside came to naught, although the record does not tell why. However, a letter from a representative of the Leighton Glass Company to FAGCO in late September, 1906, suggests what might have happened. It is pointed out that at the time the Fenton brothers came to Shadyside, Leighton was tied up in certain negotiations which made it impossible to seriously entertain FAGCO's proposals to buy. But now, in September, those negotiations had been concluded, and Leighton was anxious to sell its plant and four and one-half acres of land. Of course, the trouble with this tardy overture, was simply that FAGCO had already decided to build in Williamstown.

Although Bastow made eight trips to Williamstown, Terrell again seems to have superceded him as the company agent in finding a plant site. After the collapse of the Shadyside dealings, Terrell also went to Williamstown and met with some of the town's leading citizens and discussed the prospect of sending a committee to Martins Ferry. At length a committee composed of C. W. Dowling, prominent building contractor, W. F. Noll, a riverboat captain, and Dr. W. D. Cline, four-time mayor of the town, was chosen and authorized to visit and talk with Fenton officials in Martins Ferry. While no record of any such meeting has survived, and while no date can be established on which the decision to move to Williamstown was made, we can assume with some assurance that the Williamstown committee met with a favorable reception, and that FAGCO decided to accept its invitation in late July or early August.[4]

Another version of how the Fentons arrived in Williamstown differs substantially from what has just been described. According to this account, John was riding the streetcar to his Wheeling home one evening in the summer of 1906 when he overheard the conversation of three fellow passengers. They were discussing the misfortunes of a Williamstown man named Henderson, who had lost a lot of money in stock market speculations, and was now compelled to sell all of his property for what he could get. John allegedly passed the information along to Frank and Charles, and the three of them designated John to go to Williamstown and investigate the matter personally. John made the trip and met a local banker George P. Hunter, who advised him to see Wallace P. Beeson, a Williamstown business man. Beeson and John hit it off from the beginning and cooperated closely in purchasing the land on which to build the factory, and in organizing local operations.

The story is no doubt correct when it refers to the Henderson properties and John's collaboration with Beeson. Nothing here is inconsistent with what Terrell and a number of other people have reported. However, as far as the overheard conversation on the street car is concerned, that sounds a bit apocryphal. A further legend has it that when John first came to Marietta he was interested in purchasing the remains of the old Royal Glass Company, destroyed by fire in 1903, rather than the Henderson land. But when the owners refused to sell, he crossed the river, met Beeson, and went to work in Williamstown. This story, if true, casts doubt on all the other stories, so it must also be viewed with some skepticism.

The Henderson family first appeared in the Ohio Valley in the 1790's, but the land which the Fentons would acquire was no doubt inherited by the Hendersons later through intermarriage with the Tomlinson clan, one of Williamstown's earliest families. At any rate, by 1900, the Henderson property, amounting to nearly 2,000 acres located in and just south of Williamstown, was owned by three brothers, Jock B., Henry C., and Arthur T. The southern half of the land was individually owned, but the half nearest to town was held in common by the brothers. Shortly after the turn of the century, Henry C. "Hal" Henderson went to Gloversville, New York, and purchased a street railway line. It proved a bad investment, however, and by 1904, he was deep in debt. In order to satisfy his several creditors, Henry was now compelled to sell some of his property, and he decided to dispose of his portion of the northern half of the family's land.

An engineer in Parkersburg was appointed to survey the property and subdivide it into lots of varying sizes. The survey took about three days, and when it was completed, the individual lots were to be auctioned off to the highest bidder. The auction must have taken place some time in the summer of 1905, although the date cannot be pinpointed. A large crowd traipsed along behind the auctioneer as he moved around from lot to lot. The bidding was unusually brisk, and when it was all over, about one hundred acres of land had been sold for $36,000, an average of $360 per acre.

[4]*A May, 1907 "Glass & Pottery World" reported, in a story concerning the financing of the Fenton Brothers (probably written by John himself), "When the three glass decorators from Martins Ferry, Ohio, came down to look into the advantages for locating a glass factory, Williamstown talked a bonus or loan of $30,000. But while gas is cheap down there, 7¢ to 8¢ per thousand feet, hot air in West Virginia, as in New York, is still cheaper and harder to exchange for coin of the realm. Mr. John Fenton aided by the president of one of the banks, then took the matter into their own hands."*

A portion of the auctioned lots very shortly fell into the hands of the same Captain Noll, who would be a member of the citizens committee appointed to visit Martins Ferry. Noll may have actually acquired the lots at the auction, but that point cannot be verified. On June 1, 1906, Noll sold some seventeen acres of this old Henderson estate to G. R. and Hannah M. Hammat, who lived in nearby Vienna. The Hammats gave an option to buy the property to George W. Hunter, the banker, on July 24 for 31 days, and at the termination of that time, they extended the option until September 24. On September 15, however, "for value received," Hunter assigned all his rights and interests under the option to FAGCO. This permitted the Hammats, on the same day, to sell the seventeen acres to FAGCO for $4,769.60. The "value" which Hunter received for surrendering his option, was no doubt stock in the company, because his name appears among the shareholders in the company *Minutes.*

One might wonder why FAGCO bought so much more land than it needed on which to build a glass plant? The reason for the large purchase was simply speculation, not possession. The idea was to sell the superfluous lots, and because the factory itself would enhance the value of the lots, enough profit would accrue from the sales to finance the company in the construction of the factory and in its first months' operations in Williamstown. Hence a remunerative disposition of the lots in "The Glassworks Addition" became a matter of survival to the Fenton Art Glass Company.

In charge of the lot sales were John Fenton and Wallace P. Beeson, who had been instrumental in the decision to move to Williamstown and in the acquisition of the Henderson property. No record has survived of the dates of the sales or of the amount of land sold, but John Fenton and Beeson no doubt began disposing of the property in the latter part of September, 1906. Although company *Minutes* reveal that some of the land was still unsold by 1913, the bulk of it was probably disposed of within the first year, and perhaps within the first few months. Apparently an auctioneer was brought in from Pittsburgh to get things going, and Mr. Lem Lewis recalls how the auction began on a Saturday afternoon at the site of the future factory. "That feller from Pittsburgh"—the auctioneer—"had a great big Lincoln silk hat on . . . and you ought to have heard that boy selling them lots; he was good." Beeson and John sold many lots without the help of that "feller from Pittsburgh," but the outside auctioneer no doubt came down to "kick-off" the campaign.[5]

Ground for the new plant was broken on October 7, 1906. And though the company hoped to have the factory built and in operation before cold weather set in, as of October 15, all that had been completed was the excavation work for the furnaces and main building. On October 13, a Marietta newspaper reported that

> "The Fenton Art Glass Company is working hard on its plant and while it is advertising in several papers for help, it seems a hard matter

to get enough men to work. The Company has the surveying all done and is starting the foundations for the big plant . . . "

The labor problem remained a knotty one for on October 26 and November 2 the Marietta *Times* ran "help wanted" advertisements. Fifty laborers were needed at once at the plant site.

But things picked up in November and by the first of December the entire plant, except for the furnaces, was under shelter. John Fenton reported on the satisfactory progress of construction to the stockholders at their November 14 meeting. Work proceeded according to plan during December, and fond hopes were entertained that the company might be in production before New Year's Day. Due to an unexpected mixup, however, these hopes were not realized. It seems that some essential equipment was being shipped down from the Martins Ferry plant, but heavy fog descended on the river and navigation was suspended for two days. When the boats finally got through, someone directed them to the wharfs at Marietta, where the equipment was unloaded. It took a day or two to get the material reloaded, moved across the river, unloaded, and taken up to the plant. Consequently, the before New Years-deadline was missed, but on January 2, 1907, the first piece of glassware, a deformed cream pitcher, was taken over to the lehrs by a jubilant Charles Brand, and FAGCO's new plant was in business

The months of September, October, and November, 1906 must have been trying ones for Frank L. Fenton. Not only was he handling nearly all of the company's business in Martins Ferry, but he also had to keep in close touch with operations in Williamstown. In frequent letters to Bastow he would report on Martins Ferry affairs, ask questions about what progress Bastow was making, and suggest various types of equipment that should be purchased and ready for installation as construction progressed. A particularly disheartening development occurred only a few days after the acquisition of the Henderson land in mid-September, when the company's Martins Ferry landlord gave the Fentons a thirty-day eviction notice. Frank urged Bastow and his brother John to at least have a decorating lehr in readiness, so in the event they were dispossessed in Martins Ferry they could set something up in Williamstown. Nothing more was said of the matter, so the landlord must have relented and the company was not compelled to move out prematurely.

Construction of the factory was supposedly supervised by Bastow, although John Fenton was on the scene, and some workmen apparently thought he was the boss. When I. H. Terrell, who helped organize the Williamstown citizens committee, went to work at the plant site on October 15, 1906, as timekeeper and labor foreman, he observed that Bastow had supervised very little construction since nothing had been built. "My orders I got from J. W. Fenton," he added. Actually relations between Bastow and the Fenton brothers had cooled appreciably by this time, and Bastow was more concerned with collecting huge

[5]*The same May, 1907, "Glass & Pottery World" reported "(The) lots were chiefly taken by retired farmers, oil well operators and merchants. The price of the 50 x 150 parcels ran from $200 to $400; half down when the glass plant was started and balance when the first glass was made. No lots were offered to employees.*

The wife (sic) of most purchasers received a gorgeously decorated water set at a cost to the makers of less than fifty cents, but with the ladies happy, what investor would then hesitate about buying a $200 lot in the vicinity of one of the best equipped plants in the state and to be run by men of experience, energy and integrity."

sums of money which he thought were due him than in building a glass factory. In late October he either quit or was fired, and Jacob Rosenthal was hired in his place. Rosenthal, who was an accomplished glass-worker, chemist, and plant manager, would remain superintendant of FAGCO operations until his retirement in 1929. As we have already seen, construction shifted into high gear after November 1, which would coincide with Rosenthal's appointment as superintendent.

Early in November, 1906, shortly after he severed relations with the Fentons, Harry Bastow filed a suit in Wood County Circuit Court, charging FAGCO with breach of their oral contract with him, and demanding $15,000 in damages. The trial, held in Parkersburg, lasted from December 12 to 18, 1907. Certainly, Bastow never expected to collect $15,000, because the bill of particulars he submitted to show why Fentons owed him that much money was absurd beyond description. For his three trips to Shadyside and his services in connection therewith he demanded $300. Similarly, his professional services tied in with his eight trips to Williamstown were worth, he believed, $7,500. For designing and ordering molds he wanted $1,000; for designing the factory building he wanted $1,000; for superintending factory construction he wanted $1,000; for miscellaneous services he wanted $500. When he was finished listing these and other amounts which he thought he had coming to

him, he wound up with an un-round figure of $13,397.87. To pretty it up a bit he rounded the amount out to an even $15,000.

Frank and John Fenton denied all of Bastow's contentions and stated flatly that they did not owe him a nickel. Yet it was reported during the trial that Bastow was "an intelligent and shrewd young man" and that "it was a difficult task to entangle or confuse him." But it was also conceded that the witnesses for the defense took issue with the plaintiff on almost every point, and contradicted his testimony from beginning to end. Special attention was paid the fact that Shadyside was less than nine miles from Martins Ferry and that the one-way street railway fare between the two towns was only twenty cents. How on earth could anyone charge $300 for three trips to Shadyside? Bastow would argue that most of the charge was for his "services." The answer to this was simply that both Fentons were also present, at least on two of the trips, and they were able to exercise their own judgment on the feasibility of the move to Shadyside. Other comparable absurdities in Bastow's list were also exposed. The jury must have been quite impressed by the case for the defense, because, while finding for Bastow, it awarded him only $150, one percent of what he sued for. Neither side, according to the press, was happy with the outcome, but no appeal was made and the judgment stood.

II
EARLY YEARS IN WILLIAMSTOWN

Though founded in 1787, Williamstown had grown little in the next 120 years. When the Fentons arrived, it possessed one basket company, a wagon and buggy factory, the "Marietta Rustic Company," and about 500 citizens. People and industrial enterprises seemed to avoid it. In the early days, Williamstown was fortunate in escaping large scale Indian massacres. In later days it luckily had no criminal class, since even "men of the underworld give the place a wide berth." However, incorporated in 1901, the town was well-fixed for its own needs. It had its own water supply, purchased from Marietta and piped across the river, a bank was established in 1902, a bridge over the Ohio to Marietta ended ferry boat communication in 1903, interurban lines connected it with both Parkersburg and Marietta, natural gas provided inexpensive fuel, and water and rail transport afforded easy access to major markets. Hence, even if Williamstown was a small, undeveloped town, it had much to offer, was imbued with a strong civic spirit, and was a delightful place in which to reside. FAGCO quickly became the biggest industry, employing, in time, almost 200 people, and paying out over $2,000 in bi-weekly wages.

Before describing the organization and early operations of the new factory, it might be well to briefly outline the structure of a typical glass plant, and familiarize ourselves with some of the terms that will be used throughout this narrative. The basic components in glass are sand, soda ash, and lime. The many elaborate and beautiful colors which appear in art glass are obtained by mixing with the basic elements various combinations of metallic salts. Salts of

the different metals and the colors they produce are as follows:

Copper	Blue
Iron/chromium	Green
Sugar, iron, sulphur	Amber
Selenium and Cadmium sulfide	Orange
Neodymium and Selenium	Pink
Cobalt and Manganese	Black
Manganese	Amethyst
Aluminum and Fluorine	Milk (opal)
Gold	Cranberry
Phosphate	Opalescent

The salts are mixed into a "batch" in the mixing room and then wheeled into the "hot metal works." In this production room there is a large central furnace containing a number of separate clay "pots," plus a series of "day-tanks," small direct-fire furnaces. The FAGCO "Tour Guide Manual" describes what happens next: "The glass batch is shoveled by hand into the pot or tank. It melts at about 2500 degrees Fahrenheit. The day-tank melts glass in about 12 hours which lets us work it in the daytime, melt a new batch at night and have it ready to work the next day. Hence a 'day' tank. Glass in the pot is melted by indirect heat coming through the walls of the pot instead of direct flame on the batch as in the tank. Pot glass takes about 30 hours to melt." Pots wear out under the corrosive effect of the molten glass and must be replaced every six to eight months. Day tanks last a few months longer. Some glass, like milk glass, can be made only in day tanks, while other glasses can only be made in pot furnaces.

Changing a worn-out pot is a major operation, requiring the combined efforts of about 20 men. The old -ton pot has to be wheeled out of its niche in the main furnace, the area cleaned of glass debris, and the new pot wheeled into place. A heavy dolly has to be inserted under the old pot before it can be wheeled out, and the dolly under the new pot must be removed before the new pot can be properly installed. The manual manipulation of the dollies and pots alone is not an easy chore, but more than this, the work has to be done in the face of a blazing 2500 degree heat pouring out of the furnace opening. To protect the workers a heavy metal shade, anchored on pullies, hangs above the opening and is dropped down to cover the opening. The shade is lowered and raised as the needs of the workers demand. Generally only enough clearance is permitted to allow the men to maneuver the pot with their long steel prongs. Every few minutes the shade is dropped to the floor, allowing the workers a brief respite before the next assault on the pot.

The workers in the hot metal department are organized by "shops," the head of the shop being the presser. The system works something like this: a "gatherer" scoops up a chunk of molten glass out of the day-tank or pot and carries it on the head of an iron bar ("punty") over to his presser, where the glass drips down into the mold which sits on the press. The

presser snips off the flow of glass when a sufficient amount has gone into the mold, while the gatherer winds up the string, scrapes off the residue, and returns for another "gather." The presser meanwhile brings down the plunger suspended above the mold, which forces the molten glass out into all corners of the mold. After the plunger is withdrawn, a "carrying-over boy" seizes the glassware with a pair of tongs and sets it on a nearby stand. Here a "warming-in boy" picks up the piece in a "snap" and inserts it in a "glory hole," a small oven which softens the article just enough to permit some final changes to be made in it. The warming-in boy now takes the article of glass, still fixed to the snap, to the "finisher." laying the rod across the two broad arms of the bench on which he is seated. The finisher employs many skills "as he flares the glass, crimps it, reduces the diameter of an area of a piece to change its shape, puts the lip on a jug, straightens the stem on a footed item" and performs many other specialized tasks.

If the item requires a handle it goes from the finisher to another highly skilled workman called a "handler." Handle-gatherers bring the pieces to the handlers who "must work the glass in a very short space of time, before it sets up and cannot be shaped anymore." A "ringer" is a skilled glassworker, who "spins a thin ring of molten glass to the outer edge of each piece." The last person to handle a piece of pressed

The selecting room, circa 1907, where the glass was checked before packing—note the Coinspot pitchers at the far right of the room.

ware is the "carrying-in boy", who seizes the finished product in a paddle or fork and carries it to the annealing lehr, where it is gradually cooled to relieve any strains built up in the manufacturing process. Lehrs are long, continuous woven-metal conveyor belts which carry the pieces very slowly from the hot metal works to the Selecting Department. It takes about two hours and 20 minutes for glassware to cool as it moves along the lehr.

In addition to pressed ware, some items are made by a blowing process, in which the molten glass is forced into the mold by air pressure, supplied through a blowpipe either orally or from an air hose. The gatherer gathers the glass on a blowpipe and delivers it to the "blocker," who shapes the glass and blows the first bubble of air through the pipe. A helper next cools the piece with a blast of air and then reheats it in the glory hole. Finally, the blower manipulates the glass into the desired shape and then plunges it into the mold. He forces the glass into the recesses of the mold by blowing into the pipe, and then dexterously detaches the pipe from the glass. The ware is removed from the mold and finished in the same fashion as a piece of pressed ware.

With this sketchy account of how a glass factory operates let us examine the FAGCO structure at the time it opened its doors in January, 1907. The original one floor concrete block building was 275 feet long and 80 feet wide. Housed under this one roof were the main offices, the furnaces and lehrs, and the mixing, decorating, and packing rooms. A Baltimore and Ohio Railroad siding extended up to the loading dock adjacent to the mixing and packing rooms. The raw materials were unloaded at the mixing room, and the packed, finished products were loaded on the boxcars a short distance away from the packing room. The furnace room, or hot metal department, was 80

feet by 80 feet, in the center of which was a 12 pot furnace. Several small auxiliary buildings completed Fenton's physical plant.

Looking first at the office force, the 1907 personnel included, of course, the two Fenton brothers, John as vice-president and Frank L. as secretary and general manager. Dent and Howells, you will recall, the president and treasurer, remained in Bridgeport until resigning their posts at the end of the year. The bookkeeper was Thomas P. Butcher, who held that position until his death in 1921. Butcher had signed an agreement with the Fenton Company on January 3, 1907, by the terms of which he would purchase $1,000 worth of company stock and FAGCO, in turn, would employ him as bookkeeper at $75 per month. If his services proved unsatisfactory the company reserved the right to repurchase the stock. Butcher remained on the job even though he was not a trained or systematic bookkeeper, and even though the company's records were not in the best shape. Since he had no filing system, his desk was generally in a mess—"everything was always overlaid"—and he often spent a good bit of the day in his garden which he planted on a rented lot near the factory. Frank L. Fenton, in his easy-going fashion, permitted Butcher to carry on this way. At the end of the year—financial statements were made out annually at FAGCO for many years—it required the pooled genius of the entire force to prepare a reasonably accurate record of business operations from Butcher's jumble of figures. About the time of Butcher's death in 1921, a certified public accountant was brought in, and a new bookkeeping system was instituted, marking an end to the earlier chaos.

The first woman employee in the office was Sylvia Worster, who worked as a secretary even before the new factory was completed. During October, November, and December, 1906, while construction was going on, FAGCO used rented, upstairs offices in the Williamstown National Bank building on Williams Avenue near the Ohio River. She had at one time worked in the office of the Royal Glass Company in Marietta, so she was familiar with glass house operations. As the business grew, however, the need for another secretary-clerk arose, and in July, 1909, Grace Sayre came to work for the company, beginning a relationship which would last until here retirement 47 years later. Miss Sayre, who had graduated from high school only the year before, had been attending a business school in Marietta for about seven months, when a call was received from Frank L. Fenton for a stenographer. She got the job. Shy and bashful, tiny Grace was afraid to even ask what her wages would be; she would welcome whatever they gave her. She recalls that Sylvia Worster told someone in the plant that she would not last two weeks. Not only did she prove Miss Worster wrong, but in eight weeks she received her first pay raise.

Although Grace Sayre had no special bookkeeping experience either, she gradually eased herself into Butcher's department. By observing what he did, and did not do, she learned the rudiments of the job, which perhaps partly explains why things did not go to ruin while Butcher was tending his garden. More and more she assumed the bookkeeper's duties, and after Butcher's death, the job was logically hers.

Butcher was in his late 60's when he began working for FAGCO, so he must have been over 80 when he died. And even though he was not the world's greatest bookkeeper, he managed — with some assistance — to get along, and he remained a popular figure in the FAGCO family. William Bedillion was the shipping clerk in the early years, and he and his wife, Augusta, were stockholders in the company for quite awhile.

The Fenton plant at this time was a bit on the primitive side. There was neither running water nor electricity. A well was located near by and Sylvia Worster used to go there two or three times a day and bring back a pitcher of drinking water. Lighting was by gas, and the flooring was all wooden, which caused problems occasionally in the hot metal works. All company valuables and documents were stored temporarily in a little iron vault, which would have presented few obstacles to a polished safe-cracker.

Factory manager, or head of the hot metal department — the titles were synonymous and interchangeable — was Jacob Rosenthal, Bastow's successor during the days of plant construction. "Uncle Jake" as he was known by the younger Fentons, was born in Pittsburgh in 1854. He learned the glass-making trade in various plants in the Wheeling area, and in 1874 he married a young woman from Wheeling, Miss Susan Swager. In the next 25 years he worked in many different factories, during which time he developed exclusive formulas for a number of unusual

(continued on page 127)

Interior of Fenton office, circa 1907. The gentleman in the back room with the newspaper in his hand appears to be Frank L. Fenton. The man at the left is bookkeeper Thomas P. Butcher, and sitting next to Frank is his brother John.

14   Office, Fenton Art Glass Works.

IS IT FENTON GLASS?

Attributing the glassware shown in this book to Fenton was primarily made possible by the number of catalogues still available for study, many of which are reprinted for your enjoyment in this book. However, there were five other methods used where catalogue listings were not available. The Carnival Pattern Guide lists all **known** Fenton patterns as well as several **possible** Fenton patterns and the reason for their attribution. The following initials were used on the chart:

C — Original Catalogue
BB — Butler Brothers
RP — Reverse or Back Pattern
CPC — Color and Pattern Characteristics
H — Hartung Attribution
P — Presznick
HD — Hand
A — Author (Heacock)

1. ORIGINAL CATALOGUES AND MOLD DRAWINGS

This form of attribution is by far the easiest and the safest. However, there are some drawbacks. Some patterns, like **Buttons & Braids** and **Waterlily and Cattails** were made by more than one company, and it can sometimes be difficult to differentiate makers. Fortunately, in most cases it proves to be a fairly accurate form of attribution, and we are offering a comprehensive catalogue reprint to back us up.

2. BUTLER BROTHERS CATALOGUES —

This form of attribution was discussed in my Book 2 in considerable depth, but I will reiterate somewhat here. Butler Brothers was a wholesale outlet for most of the glass companies after 1900. In this catalogue were offered groupings of glassware, sometimes a combination of three to eight different patterns. It is an obvious conclusion that these barrels full of glass were packed by the manufacturers, not the wholesaler. Thus, if we know who

made one or two of the patterns, then it's a fair assumption that the rest of the grouping had a common origin.

3. REVERSE PATTERNS —

The Reverse or Back pattern is that which is found on the opposite side of the primary pattern. On bowls or novelties the primary pattern appears on the top surface, the reverse pattern on the underneath side. The Fenton exterior patterns are **Bearded Berry, Berry and Leaf Circle,** and **Orange Tree.** Reverse patterns have provided the necessary clues which attributed *Honeycomb with Clover, Peter Rabbit* and *Stalking Lion.*

4. PATTERN CHARACTERISTICS —

This form of attributing glass to Fenton by means of similar designs to known Fenton patterns, or by the shape of a bowl or compotes ruffled edge, can frequently prove risky. The *Persian Garden* pattern, which is similar to the *Persian Medallion* pattern, has often been incorrectly attributed to Fenton, with absolutely no other clues to back up this claim. However, it is a popular form of evidence used by previous writers, including myself, for years.

5. COLOR AND IRIDESCENCE —

This is the riskiest form of attributing carnival glass. However, it does provide corroborative evidence when it blends well with other factors. Fenton was the primary manufacturer of red carnival — however Imperial and Northwood also made red in very limited quantities. Fenton and Northwood both have distinctive lustres recognizable to advanced collectors, but I do not recommend it as bonafide evidence.

6. EARLIER ATTRIBUTIONS BY OTHER AUTHORS —

The three recognized authorities in the field of Carnival glass are Marion Hartung, Rose M. Presznick and Sherman Hand. If I concur with their beliefs that a certain pattern was made by Fenton, then I credit them with their conclusions.

FENTON CARNIVAL PATTERN GUIDE

Listed in this chart are those patterns which are known to have been made by Fenton in carnival (iridescent) glass, or those which have been attributed to Fenton by recognized authorities in this field. They are listed in alphabetical order according to their most popular name. If no name existed previously, a name was assigned to them by this author. How the pattern was attributed to Fenton is listed next according to code. If more than one name has been assigned to a pattern (why this practice persists, I will never understand), it is then listed. A cross-reference to the other key carnival glass publications is offered next. I then list the shapes in which the pattern was made, and finally where the pattern is illustrated in this book. The following abbreviations have been used in this guide;

NBA — Named by Author
A   — Author name/attribution
H   — Hartung name/attribution
HD — Hand name/attribution
P   — Presznick name/attribution
C   — Shown in original Catalogues
BB — Shown in Butler Brothers grouping
MD — Attributed from Mold Drawings
RP — Attributed by Reverse Pattern
CPC — Attributed by Color and Pattern Characteristics
N.I. — Not Illustrated

Primary Pattern Name	Att.	Other Name	Hartung	Presznick	Hand	Items Made	Illus.
ACORN (H)	C	OAK LEAF & ACORN (P) GRAPE LEAVES & ACORNS (HD)	2-90	1-134	3-45	Bowls	52
APPLE TREE	C	BANDED CRAB APPLE (P)	2-98	1-46		Water sets	37
APRIL SHOWERS (H)	C		9-14			VASES	54, 57
AUTUMN ACORN (H)	BB		3-77		3-53	Bowls	N.I.
BEARDED BERRY (H)	C		2-91			Reverse pattern of: ORANGE TREE, PETER RABBIT, PERSIAN MEDALLION, etc.	124
BANDED DRAPE (H)	C	IRIS & RIBBON (HD) PAINTED IRIS & BAND (P)	5-28	3-151	4-29	Water sets	38
BIRDS & CHERRIES (H)	C	BIRDS ON BOUGH (P)	1-111	1-17		2-hdl bon-bon, compote, rare plate, bowls	48, 51, 52
BLACKBERRY (H)	C	BLACKBERRY A. (P)	1-90	1-19		Novelties	58
BLACKBERRY BLOCK (H)	MD	BLACKBERRY AND CHECKERBOARD (P)	3-79	2-30		Water set	40

Primary Pattern Name	Att.	Other Name	Hartung	Presznick	Hand	Items Made	Page #
BLACKBERRY SPRAY (H)	C	BLACKBERRY B. (P)	1-91	1-20		Bon-bon, compote, novelties in all shapes	32, 47
BLACKBERRY BANDED (H)	C		5-57			Novelties	51, 124
BLACKBERRY BRAMBLE (H)	C		7-118			Novelties	54
BLACKBERRY MINT (H)	BB		6-105		3-23	Tiny compote, probably an individual mint dish See Presznick 4, pg. XIX	N.I.
BLUEBERRY (H)	C		2-101		2-17	Water sets	37, 40
BOUQUET (H)	H	SPRING FLOWERS (P)	2-60	1-177	3-11	Water sets	41
BUTTERFLIES (H)	BB		1-112	1-66	2-91	2-Hdl Bon-bon	51
BUTTERFLY & BERRY (H)	C	BUTTERFLY & GRAPE (P)	1-113	1-25	3-13	Complete table setting	35, 39, 42
BUTTERFLY AND FERN (H)	C	BUTTERFLY & PLUME	2-121	1-26	2-13	Water set	37
BUTTERFLY ORNAMENT (H)	A	NORTHWOOD MOTH (P)	5-100	4-134		Ornament only	78
CAPTIVE ROSE (H)	CPC	BATTENBURG LACE #2 (P)	1-24	1-14		bowls, compote, hdl. bon-bon, 6" & 9" plates	51
CARNIVAL THISTLE (H)	BB	THISTLE (P)	1-70	1-200	3-43	Bowls & plates	53
CAROLINA DOGWOOD (H)	CPC		5-59		1-47	Bowls & plates	N.I.
CHERRY, FENTON'S (H)	C	CHERRIES & MUMS (P)	4-70	2-47	2-77	Exterior pattern on MIKADO compote	45
CHERRY CHAIN (H)	C		3-80			bowls & bon-bons (O.T. or B.B. reverse)	55, 57
CHERRY CIRCLES (H)	C	CHERRIES & HOLLY WREATH (P)	2-103	1-32	2-67	2-hdl bon-bon, bowls & plates	54
CHRYSANTHEMUM (H)	CPC HD BB	WINDMILL & MUMS (HD)	2-65		2-51	10" & 11" bowls	47, 53

Primary Pattern Name	Att.	Other Name	Hartung	Presznick	Hand	Items Made	Page #
COIN DOT (H)	CPC		1-26	1-40	3-51	Re-tooled mold from FEATHER STITCH	N.I.
CONCORD (H)	C	LATTICED GRAPE (P) CONCORD GRAPE (HD)	6-58	3-121	4-71	Bowls & plates	49
COSMOS VARIANT (H)	CPC	COSMOS (HD)	5-62		2-56	Bowls	58
CORAL (H)	H		6-59		5-65	9" bowl, compote & a plate	N.I.
DAISY CUT BELL (H)	C	NEAR-CUT BELL (P)	6-123	2-178		Bell only	54
DETROIT ELK (H)		See "Elk, Detroit"	4-87			Bowl & plate	
DIAGONAL BAND (P)	CPC			2-64		Very rare water pitcher	N.I.
DIAMOND AND RIB (H)	C		1-19		5-239	Vases, jardinere, whimseys	43
DRAGON AND BERRY (H)	H P	DRAGON AND STRAWBERRY (P)	3-105	2-259	2-49	Bowls only	53
DRAGON & LOTUS (H)	C		1-114	1-58	1-49	Bowl & plate	25, 47
DRAGON'S TONGUE (H)	C		7-46			Footed 11" bowl Same feet as Stag & Holly Also Fenton #230 shade	109
DRAPERY, FENTON (NBA)	C	REVERSE DRAPE AND FLORAL (P) MAGNOLIA & DRAPE (HD)		3-166	5-165	Same shape & pattern as Figure 54, in decorated marigold carnival	N.I.
ELK, ATLANTIC CITY	A	ELK'S HEAD	4-89			Bowls & plates	56
ELK, DETROIT (ONE-EYED)	H HD	ELK'S HEAD (H)	4-89			Bowls & plates Two-Eyed variant by Millersburg	56
ELK, PARKERSBURG	A	ELK'S HEAD (H)	4-89			Bowls & plates	58
ELK BELL	A	CARNIVAL BELL (H)	4-96			Bell designed for "Atlantic City" only	56
ENAMELED PRISM BAND (P)	C	FORGET-ME-NOT (HD)		2-215	4-33	Water set	38

Primary Pattern Name	Att.	Other Name	Hartung	Presznick	Hand	Items Made	Page #
ENGRAVED GRAPES (H)	C		7-93 9-116			Water sets, vases, night set	73
FAN-TAIL (H)	RP BB	PEACOCK TAIL & DAISY (P)	5-35	3-155		Interior pattern for BUTTERFLY & BERRY bowl	35
FEATHERED SERPENT (H)	C	FEATHERED SCROLL (P)	2-38	1-65	3-49	Berry set & plate	50
FEATHER STITCH (H)	H		6-39		3-39	Bowls	58
FENTON #1576	C	CHERRIES AND BLOSSOMS (HD)			4-31	Water Set (decorated)	38
FENTONIA (H)	BB PC	DIAMOND & CABLE (P)	3-83	4-41		Water, table & berry set	36, 57
FENTONIA FRUIT (H)	C	CHERRY & SCALE (Custard Version)	7-96			Water, table & berry set (very rare in carnival)	57
FENTON RIB VASE (NBA)	C					Vase only	47
FENTON'S BASKET (H)	C	OPEN-EDGE BASKETWEAVE	8-33		2-91 3-23	Assorted novelties, bowls & plates	51, 52, 56
FENTON'S FLOWERS (H)	C		2-65			bowls, rose bowl, rare chop plate	34, 58
FENTON'S DAISY (H)	H		7-123			2-hdl bon-bon	N.I.
FENTON'S THISTLE (H)	C		2-39	2-93	2-91	Banana Boat only	49
FERN PANELS (H)	A CPC		3-64			Hat-shaped novelty	N.I.
FLORAL & GRAPE (H)	C	FLORAL & GRAPEVINE (P)	2-105	1-77	4-21	Water set	39, 41, 42
FLOWERING DILL (H)	C	MICHIGAN BEAUTY (P)	4-50	3-133		Hat-shaped novelty	103
FLOWERS & FRAMES (H)	HD	SINGLE FLOWER FRAMED (HD)	1-61		3-21	Bowls	N.I.
FLOWERS AND SPADES (H)	H	SPEAR MEDALLION AND FLOWERS (P)	5-65	3-186		Berry set	N.I.

Primary Pattern Name	Att.	Other Name	Hartung	Presznick	Hand	Items Made	Page #
FOUR FLOWERS (H)	H		1-60			Bowls	N.I.
FRENCH KNOTS (H)	A		5-37			Hat-shaped novelty	N.I.
GARLAND (H)	C		2-71			Rose bowl	51
GODDESS OF HARVEST (P)	PC			3-258		Bowl	45
GRAPE & CABLE, FENTON'S	C				2-35 3-31	Footed orange bowl, bowls & footed plates	50, 52, 59
GRAPEVINE LATTICE (H)	HD	GRAPEVINE DIAMOND (P)	2-72	1-94	4-19	Water Set	N.I.
HEART & HORSESHOE (H)	H	FENTON'S GOOD LUCK (HD)	3-119		5-72	Bowls & plates	54
HEART AND VINE (H)	H		2-93		3-57	Bowls and plates	46
HEARTS AND TREES (H)	C		5-39			Interior pattern of BUTTERFLY & BERRY bowls	57
HEAVY HOBNAIL (H)	C		8-35			Vases	25
HOLLY, CARNIVAL (H)	C	HOLLY & BERRY (P)	1-83	1-103	2-59 3-46	Bowls, plates, compote and hat-shaped novelty	49, 54
HONEYCOMB & CLOVER (H)	RP C	HONEYCOMB & FOUR LEAF CLOVER (P)	2-73	4-85 1-107		Bon-Bon Exterior pattern FEATHERED SERPENT	50
HORSE MEDALLION (P)	C	HORSES' HEADS (H)	1-115	1-109	1-26 1-71	Bowls, plates, rose bowl	48
ILLUSION (H)	H	FENTON'S ARABIC (P)	5-67	3-63		Bon-bon, bowls	53
IRIS (H)	BB MD		2-74	2-186	3-75	Compote, buttermilk goblet	58
JARDINIERE (H) (Note Spelling)	C	DIAMOND AND RIB (H)	5-114		2-97 3-1	Same mold made into tall vase and whimseys	43
KITTENS (H)	C		1-116	1-116	3-55 4-97	Toy-size bowls, cup/ saucers, spooner, vase, very rare cuspidor	55

Primary Pattern Name	Att.	Other Name	Hartung	Presznick	Hand	Items Made	Page #
KNOTTED BEADS (H)	C		4-13			Vase	125
LATTICE AND DAISY (H)	C	DAISY & LATTICE BAND (P)	2-75	1-51		Water set, rare berry set	41, 122
LATTICE AND GRAPE (H)	C	LATTICE & GRAPEVINE (P) GRAPE & LATTICE (HD)	1-97	1-184	3-9	Water set, rare bowls	39, 41
LEAF CHAIN (H)	C	LEAF MEDALLION (P)	2-76	1-185		Bon-bon, 9" bowls & plate	51
LEAF TIERS (H)	C	STIPPLED LEAF (P)	3-68	2-251	4-25	Water, table & berry set	36
LILY-OF-THE-VALLEY (H)	MD	BANDED LILY OF THE VALLEY (P)	5-68	3-4		Water set	39
LIONS (H)	RP BB	STALKING LION (NBA) In Custard	2-125	1-120	1-24	Bowls and plates BERRY & LEAF CIRCLE Reverse Pattern	51, 53
LITTLE DAISIES (H)	CPC		10-97			Bowls	N.I.
LITTLE FISHES (H)	C	SEA LANES (P)	2-126	1-170	2-51	Footed bowls	48
LITTLE FLOWERS (H)	C	STIPPLED DIAMOND & FLOWER (P)	1-62	1-183	5-217	Bowls, plates	49, 52
LOTUS AND GRAPE (H)	H	GRAPE & LOTUS (HD) RUFFLED MAGNOLIA & GRAPE (P)	2-113	3-177	3-49	Bon-bon, 9" bowls and plates, wine glass Variant also made	52, 102
MIKADO (H)	C		4-57		2-77	High compote only	44
MILADY (H)	C	PANELLED BACHELOR BUTTONS (P)	2-79	1-142		Water set	37, 40
MIRRORED LOTUS (H)	RP		3-69			Bowls BERRY & LEAF CIRCLE Reverse pattern	N.I.
NORTHERN STAR (H)	C		4-29			Bowls, plates	100
ORANGE TREE SMALL ORANGE TREE FOOTED SMALL O.T.	C		1-100 1-102 8-61	1-138	2-67 3-21 4-23	COMPLETE SET	33-34 42, 45 46, 58 122, 123
ORANGE TREE & SCROLL (P)	H	ORANGE TREE, VARIENT (H)	4-74	2-192		Water set	58

Primary Pattern Name	Att.	Other Name	Hartung	Presznick	Hand	Items Made	Page #
ORANGE TREE ORCHARD (H)	C	ORANGE TREE & CABLE (P) CABLE (P)	7-107	1-138		Water set	34
PANTHER (H)	C			1-117		Berry Bowl & sauces	29, 35, 48
PANELLED DANDELION (H)	BB MD	DANDELION, VARIANT	3-88	2-63	2-19	Water set	37
PEACOCK (FLUFFY BIRD)	C	FLUFFY PEACOCK (A)	3-106	2-201	2-11	Water set	37, 40
PEACOCK AND DAHLIA (H)	C			2-127		Bowls & plates	53
PEACOCK AND GRAPES (H)	BB			2-128	1-151	1-14 2-63	Bowls & plates	53
PEACOCK & URN (H)	RP BB			1-134	1-152	1-18	Bowls	48, 60
PEACOCK TAIL (H)	C	FLOWERING ALMONDS (P)	1-37	1-79		Bowls, compote, hat-shaped novelty	54, 55, 56 57, 59
PERSIAN MEDALLION (H)	C			1-40	1-153	1-73 2-40	2-hdl bon-bon, compote, rose bowl, bowls & plates	44, 47, 51
PETER RABBIT (H)	RP			4-108	3-157	2-39	Bowls & plates	46
PINE CONE (H)	C	PINE CONE WREATH (P)	2-96	1-154	3-45	Bowls & plates	49
PLAID (H)	BB	GRANNY'S GINGHAM (P)	4-34	3-86		Bowls & plates	49
POND LILY (H)	C			4-59			2-hdl bon-bon	54
PRAYER RUG (H)	C			8-45			Bon-bon	121
PRISM BAND, ENAMELLED (P)	C	THREE BAND (P)		2-215 3-204	4-33	Water set	38
RAGGED ROBIN (H)	BB			5-75			Bowls	125
RIB & HOLLY SPRIG (A)	C						Compotes	122

Primary Pattern Name	Att.	Other Name	Hartung	Presznick	Hand	Items Made	Page #
RIBBON TIE (H)	BB	COMET (P)	3-90	1-213		Bowls	50, 52
ROSE TREE (H)	RP		7-138		5-69	Bowl O.T. Reverse Pattern	N.I.
RUSTIC VASE (H)	C	MARYLAND (P)	2-27	1-127		2 Sizes of vases	54
SAILBOATS (H)	C	SAILBOAT & WINDMILL (P)	1-86	1-169	3-75	Bowls, goblets & wines, high-stem compote	51, 53, 57
SCALE BAND (H)	C MD	TWO BAND (P)	3-93	2-283		Bowls & plates, pitcher and tumblers	40
SOLDIERS AND SAILORS (H)	RP		4-94			Plate BERRY & LEAF CIRCLE Reverse Pattern	56
STAG AND HOLLY (H)	BB C		1-124		3-17 1-24	Bowls & plates of all sizes and shapes	44, 48
STIPPLED RAYS (H)	C		1-32			2-hdl bon-bon, bowls and plates	59
STRAWBERRY (H)	C		2-117			2-hdl bon-bon	49
STRAWBERRY SCROLL (H)	MD	STRAWBERRY AND SCROLL BAND (P)	5-77	2-260	4-17	Water set	40
STREAM OF HEARTS (H)	RP		8-49			Compote	53
SWAN (Novelty)	C	PASTEL SWAN (H)	3-125		2-83	Novelty	55
TEN MUMS (H)	C	DOUBLE CHRYSANTHEMUM (P) CHRYSANTHEMUM WREATH (P)	3-73	2-51 2-75	2-49 3-7	Water set, bowls	38, 41 49
THISTLE AND LOTUS (H)	RP BB		6-71			7" Bowl	N.I.
TWO FLOWERS (H)	C	DOGWOOD & MARSH LILY (P)	1-72	1-57	1-33 2-59	7" & 10" footed bowls	49
TWO FRUITS (H)	C	APPLE & PEAR (P)	1-105	2-4		Divided bon-bon	58
VINTAGE (H)	C	GRAPE DELIGHT (P)	1-106	4-113	3-63	Tiny epergne, bowls and plates, fernery	50, 52, 55 126

Primary Pattern Name	Att.	Other Name	Hartung	Presznick	Hand	Items Made	Page #
WATER LILY (H)	C	MAGNOLIA & POINSETTIA (P) LOTUS & POINSETTIA (HD)	1-73	2-163	2-36	Footed bowls	49, 55
WATER LILY & CATTAILS (H)	C	CATTAILS & WATER LILY (P)	1-74	1-30	2-99	Banana Boat (exterior pattern)	49
WILD BLACKBERRY (H)	CPC		5-80			Bowls	N.I.
WINE AND ROSES (H)	C	CABBAGE ROSE AND GRAPE (P)	7-113	2-41	3-73	Pitcher and wines	41
WREATH OF ROSES (H)	C	ROSE WREATH (HD) AMERICAN BEAUTY ROSES (P)	1-77	1-4	2-33 3-25	2-hdl compote, punch bowl and cups	44, 45 46, 52, 54 126
ZIG-ZAG (H)	C		9-124		4-35	Water set (decorated)	38, 39, 57

COLORS IN CARNIVAL GLASS

As a specialist in historical documentation of colored glass production, I have learned that attempting to name all colors in which a pattern can be found is sometimes risky. I often get letters from readers informing me of unlisted colors or decorations, which I am certain were produced under extremely limited circumstances. Naturally, all patterns had primary colors in which they were manufactured or decorated, but on occasion—for reasons about which we can only speculate—items appear on the market today in previously unlisted colors.

This is especially true when one is listing colors in carnival glass. Each pattern and novelty was made in from two to four primary colors, but rare experimental colors are always appearing at auctions, causing heated bidding among collectors so anxious to own the rarer colors of their favorite patterns.

Thus, I have made no attempt to list the colors in which each of Fenton's patterns were made. Instead, I am listing here all known colors made in carnival glass, bearing in mind that each color listed has varying degrees of depth and clarity.

When one is listing colors of iridescent glass, you must also take into consideration that when the coating of iridescence was applied and fired, quite often the glass took on an entirely different appearance. You actually have to hold the item up against a bright light to see the "base" color. Sometimes the base color is very pale, but the iridescence so sharp that the item has a very rich appearance.

VIVID COLORS

RICH MARIGOLD—An almost red-orange shade
MARIGOLD—A yellow-orange shade
BLUE—from very pale to deep cobalt
COBALT BLUE—the deepest and most desirable shade of blue
AMETHYST (PURPLE)—from very pale to a rich deep purple
RED—A deep red when held to a light
AMBERINA—a deep red blending into yellow-gold
GREEN—from a light yellow-green to a rich emerald color

PASTELS

WHITE—Frosty crystal with rainbow iridescence
CLEAR—Unfrosted crystal with iridescence
CLAMBROTH—Just a touch of amber
SMOKY—Just a touch of grey
AQUA—pale blue (sometimes with opalescence), often coated with amber-gold iridescence
GREEN—a delicate lime green
VASELINE—often called chartreuse, a definite yellow-green
ICE BLUE—a light, frosty blue

Fenton Glass in Color

A
Rustic Hobnail

B
Dancing Ladies

C
Waterlily & Cattails

D
Leaf Tiers

E
Dragon & Lotus

Illustrated above are five truly unique items in early Fenton glass. Figure A is Fenton's #517 mold which was usually "swung" into a tall 21" vase (see page 104). Hartung calls this *Heavy Hobnail* (Book 8) and believes it was meant to hold combs in a barber shop. It is shown here in clear carnival. Figure B is the #901 *Dancing Ladies*, 16" covered urn in a custard color originally called "Chinese Yellow" by Fenton. This piece dates circa 1933. The Figure C *Waterlily and Cattails* water pitcher is quite rare in the amethyst opalescent color, and dates about 1908. It was also made in opalescent blue, green and white, carnival colors, chocolate glass, and plain or frosted crystal. Figure D is a scarce #1790 *Leaf Tiers* cake plate in plain amethyst glass, which dates about 1933. It can also be found in carnival colors, red slag (Mandarin Red), opalescent white, and in milk glass (see page 112). Finally, we illustrate the Figure E *Dragon and Lotus* bowl in a very rare vaseline opalescent carnival glass. Pieces of amethyst opalescent Fenton carnival glass have also been reported. These colors are extremely rare and undoubtedly experimental. This bowl has a characteristic ribbon-candy edge.

Karnak Red Art Glass

1
21" Footed Vase

2
20" Vase

3
15" Footed Vase

4
8½" Footed Bowl

5
7" Handled Vase

In 1925, a shop of glassworkers from Europe who were skillful in the methods of offhand art glass, came to Fenton after previously working for other glass companies in the United States, including Durand and Imperial. These men worked for Fenton approximately one year, leaving when management found the market for this ware was quite limited. The color of this very rare form of art glass shown here is called Karnak Red. (This glass was also made in colors of Oriental Ivory, Antique Green & Turquoise Blue.) The 21" vase shown here originally sold for $100 in 1926, a considerable amount of money at the time. See ad reprint, page 95.

(FIG. 1) Fenton #3024-1 footed vase;

(FIG. 2) Massive 20" vase;

(FIG. 3) #3024 footed vase;

(FIG. 4) #3026 footed bowl;

(FIG. 5) #3010 handled vase.

Fenton Art Glass

7
16" Footed Vase

6
9½" Vase

8
13" Vase

9
12" Candlestick

10
12" Candlestick

11
Large Bowl

12
10½" Vase

13
9½" Candleholder

(FIG. 6) HANGING HEART vase, Fenton #3007;
(FIG. 7) HANGING VINE vase, #3024;
(FIG. 8) HANGING HEART vase, #3020;
(FIG. 9) HANGING HEART candlestick, #3018;
(FIG. 10) PULLED FEATHER candlestick, #3019;

(FIG. 11) HANGING VINE bowl;
(FIG. 12) Experimental 10½" vase, one-of-a-kind item which rested in the Fenton family library for many years;
(FIG. 13) Experimental candlestick, not a production item.

27

14
10" Vase

15
10" Vase

16
Large Crimped Vase

17
10½" Vase

18
6¾" Vase

19
Pig Whimsey

20
8" Vase

21
Wall Vase

22
Oval Compote

(FIG. 14) MOSAIC Inlaid vase, Fenton #3006;

(FIG. 15) Non-mosaic, the oddly shaded color of red was not mass-produced, but is the same shape as Figure 14;

(FIG. 16) This large piece of cranberry was made in 1915 in a pattern called RIB OPTIC by it's maker;

(FIG. 17) Mosaic Inlaid vase, not threaded, Fenton #3051;

(FIG. 18) Mosaic Inlaid #3002 vase;

(FIG. 19) This pig-shaped whimsey is a one-of-a-kind novelty made by employee Fritz Alberg;

(FIG. 20) Fenton #3024 vase;

(FIG. 21) Unusual wall vase in Fenton #3043;

(FIG. 22) Oval-shaped compote in #3055, threaded mosaic inlaid glass.

Chocolate Glass

23
Tumbler

24
Pitcher

Panther
9½" Berry

Waterlily & Cattails

26
Butter

27
Sugar

28
Creamer

29
Spooner

Waterlily & Cattails

30
Vintage
Fern Dish

31
Waterlily & Cattails
4" Berry

CHOCOLATE GLASS

Also known as caramel slag, the man who invented this unique form of colored glass was related to the Fenton family. His name was Jacob Rosenthal. He developed the formula for chocolate glass as a chemist for the Indiana Tumbler & Goblet Co., at Greentown, Indiana, and shared the secret on a limited basis with a few other factories. See notes concerning Rosenthal on page 16.

(FIG. 23-24) Fenton #8 WATERLILY & CATTAILS tumbler and water pitcher—circa 1907;

(FIG. 25) Very rare PANTHER bowl, with BUTTERFLY & BERRY exterior—this piece has a rim very much like the Greentown "Golden Agate";

(FIG. 26-29, 31) Table set and berry sauce in WATERLILY & CATTAILS;

(FIG. 30) VINTAGE fern dish, #922 pattern, circa 1910.

32
Northwood Tumbler & Pitcher

33

34
Tumbler

35
Pitcher

36
Tumbler

37
Tumbler

38
Northwood
Tumbler

39
Fenton
Tumbler

40
Spooner

41
Creamer

42
Large Crimped Bowl

43
Gravy

44
Sugar

(FIG. 32-33) Northwood version of WATERLILY & CATTAILS pattern, with trademark;

(FIG. 34-37) Fenton #8 version of this pattern, circa 1908, with three different tumblers—on Fig. 34 the tips of the cattails are apart, on Fig. 36 they overlap, on Fig. 37 they meet. The cattails on the Northwood tumbler are thinner, and there is no basket-weave pattern at the base. It is my belief that Northwood made only a water set in this pattern, and no table set or berry set.

(FIG. 38-39) Opalescent version of a Northwood and Fenton tumbler;

(FIG. 40-41) Spooner and creamer—so often seen, it is likely that they were commercially produced as a creamer and open sugar;

(FIG. 42) Amethyst opalescent crimped bowl—this color most definitely Fenton;

(FIG. 43) Novelty gravy boat formed from creamer mold;

(FIG. 44) Very rare amethyst opalescent covered sugar bowl.

45

46

Buttons & Braids
(Lemonade Set)

47   **48**   *Honeycomb & Clover*   **49**   **50**
(Table Set)

51

Waterlily & Cattails
(Tumbler)

52

Honeycomb & Clover
(Butter)

53

Fenton Drapery
(Tumbler)

(FIG. 45-46) BUTTONS AND BRAIDS, Fenton's #351, with pressed tumbler and mold-blown pitcher—circa 1910. This pattern was also made by Jefferson Glass Company, with a blown tumbler;

(FIG. 47-50) HONEYCOMB WITH CLOVER, which can now be attributed to Fenton, as this pattern was used on the exterior of their #437, "Feathered Serpent" bowl—circa 1909;

(FIG. 51) WATERLILY AND CATTAILS, Fenton #8, green opalescent tumbler;

(FIG. 52) Very rare green opalescent butter in HONEYCOMB AND CLOVER;

(FIG. 53) FENTON DRAPERY, #350 pattern, pressed tumbler in green opalescent—a tumbler was also made in a pressed version of Coinspot.

Fenton Opalescent

54
Fenton Drapery
(Pitcher)

55
Fenton Basket
(Flared Nappy)

56
Lattice & Daisy
(Tumbler)

57

58
Late Coinspot
(Iced Tea Set)

59
Blackberry

61
Honeycomb & Clover
(Master Berry)

61

62
Honeycomb & Clover
(Spooner & Creamer)

63
Waterlily & Cattails
(2-Handle Bon-Bon)

64

65
Fenton Basket
(3-Toed Console Set)

(FIG. 54) FENTON DRAPERY, #350 pattern, mold-blown water pitcher;

(FIG. 55) FENTON BASKET, #1092 pattern, flared nappy, circa 1911;

(FIG. 56) Rare vaseline opalescent LATTICE AND DAISY tumbler, circa 1912—extremely limited production in opalescent;

(FIG. 57-58) LATE COINSPOT, #1352 pattern, pitcher with ice lip and tumbler, circa 1929;

(FIG. 59) BLACKBERRY SPRAY nappy, in typical Fenton amethyst opalescent;

(FIG. 60) Master berry bowl in HONEYCOMB & CLOVER;

(FIG. 61-62) Same in spooner and creamer, blue opalescent;

(FIG. 63) WATERLILY & CATTAILS 2-handled bon-bon in unusual pale blue;

(FIG. 64-65) #1093 FENTON BASKET console set, circa 1930, in green opalescent.

Orange Tree

66
Tumbler

67
Pitcher
(No Scales)

68
Hatpin Holder

69
Puff Box

70
Punch Bowl

71
Spooner

72
Butter

73
Sugar

74
Creamer

75
Breakfast Sugar

76
Breakfast Creamer

77
Orange Bowl

The ORANGE TREE pattern family has been variously named *Small Orange Tree, Footed Small Orange Tree,* even "Fenton Flowers", but they all fall under the same family name, so most collectors refer to all pieces simply as Orange Tree. The pattern was made about 1911, and due to it's popularity, was produced for several years thereafter. Fenton even designed another pattern with a similar motif, called ORANGE TREE ORCHARD (Fig. 81-82).

(FIG. 66-67) Fenton #1402 water set;
(FIG. 68) #1410 Hatpin holder;
(FIG. 69) #1403 covered puff box;
(FIG. 70) #1400 punch bowl;
(FIG. 71-74) #1402 table set;
(FIG. 75-76) #1411 breakfast set;
(FIG. 77) #921 Orange bowl.

Orange Tree
(And other related patterns)

78
Pitcher
(with scales)

79
Tumbler

80
Punch Bowl

81

82

Orange Tree Orchard
(Tumbler & Pitcher)

83
Loving Cup

84
Loving Cup

85
Loving Cup

86
Nut Bowl
("Fenton Flowers")

87
Wine

88
9" Plate

89
Shaving Mug

90
8" Berry Dish

(FIG. 78-79) Note the difference between this pitcher and the Figure 67 example. This one has the distinctive Fenton "scales", whereas the other does not. The tumbler is rare without scales;

(FIG. 80) Same as Figure 70, except in green;

(FIG. 81-82) Cobalt blue Fenton #6 ORANGE TREE ORCHARD water pitcher and tumbler, circa 1912;

(FIG. 83-85) #1413 Loving Cup in green, purple and blue;

(FIG. 86) Those look like orange trees to me, but this one often carries the name FENTON FLOWERS—Fenton #1401 marigold nut bowl, circa 1911;

(FIG. 87) #1412 marigold wine glass;

(FIG. 88) #1406 Blue 9" plate;

(FIG. 89) #1430 red mug, probably for shaving;

(FIG. 90) #1406 red "grape" dish, not part of a set; note BEARDED BERRY reverse pattern.

Butterfly & Berry

91 Tumbler

92 Pitcher

93 Hatpin Holder

94 10" Swung Vase

95 10" Swung Vase

96 Sugar

97 Creamer

98 Butter

99 Spooner

100 Master Berry

101 Indiv. Berry ("Panther" Interior)

102 Master Berry ("Fantail" Interior)

BUTTERFLY AND BERRY was another popular line put out by Fenton around 1911 in a complete table setting. It was their #1124 pattern, made primarily in blue and marigold, less often in green and purple. Two rare examples of the berry bowl are shown in this book in white carnival and in chocolate glass. An interesting feature about the berry bowls is that they accommodate four different interior patterns—the standard wreath of grapes (Fig. 100), the PANTHER, the HEARTS & TREES (Fig. 296), and the FANTAIL. All pieces, except Figure 95, are in blue or cobalt blue.

(FIG. 91-92) Tumbler and pitcher in blue;

(FIG. 93) Blue hatpin holder;

(FIG. 94-95) 10" pulled (or swung) vases in blue and red, made from tumbler mold;

(FIG. 96-99) 4-piece table set;

(FIG. 100) Master berry with standard interior design;

(FIG. 101) #1125 individual berry (or nappy), with PANTHER;

(FIG. 102) #1126 master berry bowl with FANTAIL pattern interior. Note the smaller size and shorter feet in comparison to Figure 100.

Fentonia & Leaf Tiers

103
Tumbler

104
Pitcher

105
Tumbler

106
Pitcher

107
Spooner

108
Butter

109
Sugar

110
Creamer

111
Butter

112
Sugar

113
Creamer

114
Spooner

Pictured above are two patterns also available in a complete set for setting the table. There is no documentative proof that FENTONIA (FIGS. 103-104, 111-114) was made by Fenton, except that it is almost identical to FENTONIA FRUIT (FIG. 295), which was their #1134 pattern. Oddly enough, it is the rarer of the two patterns which shows up in existing catalogues. FENTONIA dates around 1913-1915.

LEAF TIERS (FIGS. 105-110) was Fenton's #1790 pattern, made primarily in marigold, and very rare in dark carnival (green, blue, purple). Note the distinct branch-like feet which match those on the Figure 86 nut bowl. The mold drawings date this beginning in 1914.

115   116
Milady

117   118
Fluffy Peacock

119   120
Panelled Dandelion

121   122   123
Blueberry

124
Apple Tree

125   126
Butterfly & Fern

(FIG. 115-116) MILADY pitcher and tumbler in cobalt, Fenton's #1110 pattern, circa 1910;

(FIG. 117-118) Amethyst #1109 PEACOCK or FLUFFY PEACOCK (I prefer the latter) pitcher and tumbler in purple. This has been incorrectly attributed to Millersburg;

(FIG. 119-120) Amethyst PANELLED DANDELION pitcher and tumbler, circa 1910, with attribution based on Butler Brothers catalogue for that year, mold drawings confirm this attribution.

(FIG. 121-122) #1562 BLUEBERRY pattern pitcher and tumbler in cobalt blue;

(FIG. 123-124) #124 APPLE TREE pitcher and tumbler in cobalt blue. The mold for this pitcher was later revived in the thirties and reproduced in opalescent colors and milk glass (without a handle in the form of a vase);

(FIG. 125-126) #910 BUTTERFLY AND FERN pattern pitcher and tumbler in green—also made in many other colors.

127   128   129   130   131   132
Banded Drape   *Ten Mums*   *Prism Band*

133   134   135   136   137
Zig-Zag   *Bouquet*

Fenton #1576
("Cherries & Blossoms")

(FIG. 127-128) #1016 BANDED DRAPE lemonade pitcher and tumbler with Iris decoration;

(FIG. 129-130) Attribution of the TEN MUMS pitcher and tumbler is based upon the nearly identical design used on their #1057 bowl (see catalogue reprint, page 83), and a mold drawing dated 1912. It is known in marigold, blue and white and is quite scarce in the water set;

(FIG. 131-132) Fenton's #1014 Lemonade pitcher and tumbler known today as Enameled PRISM BAND. The tumbler mold was also used for the Banded Drape pattern. See the catalogue reprint, page 81;

(FIG. 133) ZIG-ZAG pitcher, Fenton's #1015, which also takes a "Prism Band" tumbler (see page 81), made in all colors;

(FIG. 134-135) BOUQUET pattern tumbler and pitcher, attributed by most to Fenton because of pattern design and color—does not appear in existing catalogues which are available, so I estimate production at around 1914;

(FIG. 136-137) Fenton's #1576 (mold), CHERRIES & BLOSSOMS enamel-decorated tumbler and pitcher—same mold used on decorated non-iridescent colored glass. See ad reprint, page 101. This pitcher is often referred to as the Cannonball pitcher.

More Pitchers & Tumblers

138
Floral & Grape

139
Lily-of-the-Valley

140
Lattice & Grape

141 **142**
Butterfly & Berry

143 **144**
Zig-Zag

(FIG. 138) This Floral & Grape pitcher was made by Dugan-Diamond, circa 1915. Note the ribs lean to the left. The Floral & Grape Variant shown on page 81 was made by Fenton, with the ribs leaning to the right. See also page 118.

(FIG. 139) 1912 mold drawings concur with the speculative Fenton attribution offered by most carnival authorities on this LILY-OF-THE-VALLEY pattern, which is extremely rare.

(FIG. 140) Fenton's #1563 LATTICE AND GRAPE pitcher, scarce in dark carnival, circa 1912;

(FIG. 141-142) Green carnival version of popular BUTTERFLY & BERRY, #1124 pattern, circa 1911;

(FIG. 143-144) Fenton #1015 ZIG-ZAG pattern pitcher and tumbler (from PRISM BAND mold), circa 1910.

39

145   **146**
Blackberry Block

147   **148**
Milady

149   **150**
Fluffy Peacock

151
Scale Band

152
Blueberry **153**

154
Strawberry Scroll

(FIG. 145-146) BLACKBERRY BLOCK pitcher and tumbler—attribution on this is based on mold drawings dated 1908 or 1909.

(FIG. 147-148) Fenton #1110 MILADY pattern tumbler and pitcher—circa 1911;

(FIG. 149-150) PEACOCK or ELUFFY PEACOCK, #1109 pattern, circa 1910;

(FIG. 151) Fenton #212 SCALE BAND water pitcher, circa 1908;

(FIG. 152-153) Fenton #1562 BLUEBERRY pattern tumbler and pitcher—circa 1912;

(FIG. 154) Most authorities feel certain that STRAWBERRY SCROLL is a Fenton product, with estimated production about 1912—rare in dark carnival colors; mold drawings confirm date and attribution.

155   156
Lattice & Grape

157   158
Lattice & Daisy

159   160
Ten Mums

161   162
Floral & Grape

163   164
Wine & Roses

165   166
Bouquet

(FIG. 155-156) Fenton #1563 LATTICE AND GRAPE pitcher and tumbler;

(FIG. 157-158) Lattice & Daisy is a Dugan pattern, not Fenton. 1915 Butler Bros. catalogue shows Dugan's Floral & Grape with the Lattice & Daisy pitcher. Also, shards have been found at the Dugan-Diamond factory site. See pg. 118.

(FIG. 159-160) TEN MUMS pitcher and tumbler;

(FIG. 161-162) Dugan's Floral & Grape. Eight petals on the daisy and ribs lean to the left. See page 81.

(FIG. 172-173) Dugan's Floral & Grape pitcher and tumbler. See page 81.

(Fig. 165-166) BOUQUET pattern pitcher and tumbler.

Prism Band

167   168   169   170   171

Orange Tree
(Punch Bowl)

Orange Tree

172   173   174   175

Floral & Grape   (Master Berry) *Orange Tree* (Punch Cup)

176

Fenton No: 349
(11" Flared Bowl)

177

Butterfly & Berry
(Master Berry)

(FIG. 167-168) Fenton's #1014 enamelled PRISM BAND pitcher and plain tumbler. The tumbler lacks the ribbed band in the mold. Dark carnival would be rare with this flower;

(FIG. 169) punch bowl in Fenton #1400 ORANGE TREE;

(FIG. 170-171) Fenton #1402 ORANGE TREE water set;

(FIG. 172-173) Dugan's Floral & Grape pitcher and tumbler. See page 81.

(FIG. 174) Master berry bowl in ORANGE TREE; see Fig. 307;

(FIG. 175) Punch cup in ORANGE TREE;

(FIG. 176) FENTON #349, 11" flared bowl—this is not actually carnival glass, it is iridescent stretch glass, originally called "Persian Pearl";

(FIG. 177) Fenton's #1124 BUTTERFLY AND BERRY master berry bowl. There are two sizes of large berry bowls.

Diamond & Rib

178
11½" Swung Vase
(In Original Mold)

179
Jardiniere

180
21" Swung Vase

As inappropriate as the above name proves to be, I will not attempt to change it here. Figure 179 is known by some simply as "Jardinicre", but this same mold was stretched into the incredibly tall 21" vase shown as Figure #180, so I believe it should at least carry a pattern name.

Figure #178 was Fenton's #504 pattern, appearing in the catalogue shown on page 83.

The vase in the mold was only about 4½" high when it originally left the mold. The piece of glass was then attached to a long punty and "warmed in" at the glory hole by a warming-in boy, who then turned around and swung the piece in giant arcs much like a baton twirler. Centrifugal force stretched the glass piece into a vase, and when it was about 11½" tall, the swinging was stopped.

181
Wreath of Roses
("Persian Medallion" Interior)

182
Mikado
("Fenton Cherries" Exterior)

183
Stag & Holly

(FIG. 181) Fenton #1049 WREATH OF ROSES cobalt blue two-piece punch bowl with PERSIAN MEDALLION pattern interior. The punch cups to this bowl are very rare;

(FIG. 182) The interior pattern of this cobalt blue high-standard compote is called MIKADO (Fenton's #919), the exterior pattern "Fenton Cherries", it dates circa 1912. This is the only mold in which both of these patterns can be found; the same mold was formed into a cakestand.

(FIG. 183) An exceptional example of superior cobalt color and iridescence in this popular Fenton #1608 pattern known as STAG AND HOLLY, which dates around 1912. There is also a #1606 variant with spade-like feet, shown in the catalogue reprint on page 102.

182

Fenton Cherry

("Mikado" Interior)

184

Goddess of Harvest

181

Wreath of Roses

186

Orange Tree

(Punch Set)

185

(FIG. 182) Also shown on page 44, photographed again here to show exterior pattern to better advantage. Note the similarities between this and the CHERRY CIRCLES and CHERRY CHAIN patterns shown on page 54 and 55;

(FIG. 184) This extremely rare example of amethyst carnival is one of less than a dozen known. The Fenton attribution is based upon color, iridescence, pattern characteristics and the "ribbon candy" edge (identical to Figure 212, 222, 225 and 256);

(FIG. 181) Shown again here for better study of the exterior pattern—see also page 44;

(FIG. 185-186) Blue ORANGE TREE punch set—see also pages 33 and 34.

45

187
Heart & Vine

188
Wreath of Roses
(Punch Set)

189
Peter Rabbit
("Bearded Berry" Exterior)

(FIG. 187) HEART AND VINE plate in blue with superior iridescence, which makes it appear to be purple;

(FIG. 188) WREATH OF ROSES green punch set with VINTAGE pattern interior, Fenton's #469 and 1049, which also appeared in a 1910 Butler Brothers catalogue;

(FIG. 189) PETER RABBIT bowl, rare in marigold, very rare in dark carnival—with attribution based on the BEARDED BERRY exterior pattern.

Red & Amberina Carnival

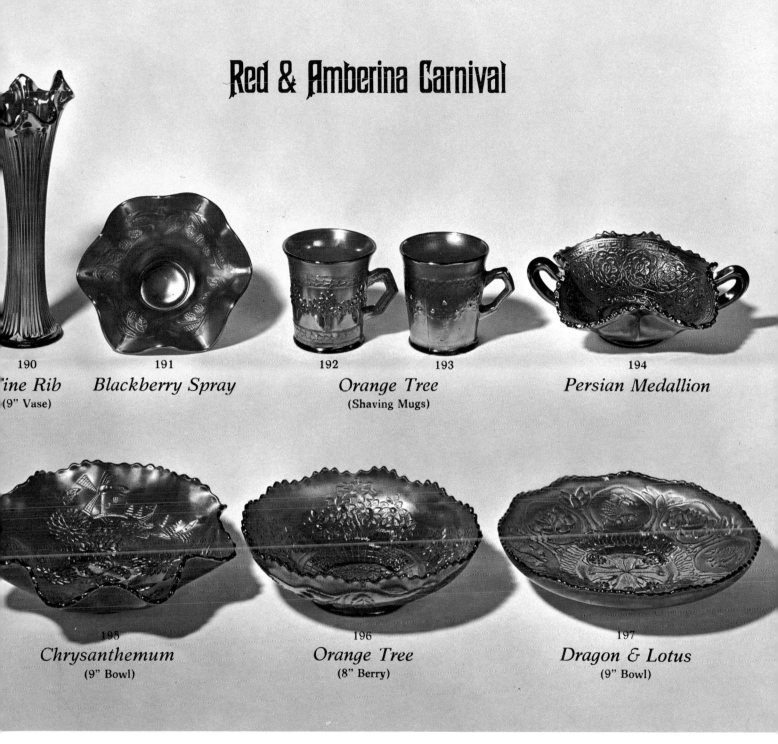

190
ine Rib
(9" Vase)

191
Blackberry Spray

192   193
Orange Tree
(Shaving Mugs)

194
Persian Medallion

195
Chrysanthemum
(9" Bowl)

196
Orange Tree
(8" Berry)

197
Dragon & Lotus
(9" Bowl)

Since red carnival is so scarce today, it is an obvious conclusion that very little was produced originally. Fenton was the primary producer of red carnival, and it is my personal conclusion that it came close to the end of the carnival glass era, circa 1925, when the formula for their ruby red pressed glass came into general use. This would explain why there is so little of it made, and also why it was made only in novelties (not sets) and only in the more popular patterns. If the red blends into a yellow base, it should be referred to as amberina carnival. Care should be taken not to confuse this color with some of the shades of deep purple carnival which have strong red highlights. The dates listed below were when the patterns were originally produced, not necessarily when the actual red pieces were made.

(FIG. 190) Fenton's #1126 FINE RIB vase, circa 1910;

(FIG. 191) Fenton #1216 BLACKBERRY SPRAY flared bon-bon, circa 1911;

(FIG. 192-193) Fenton #1430 ORANGE TREE shaving mugs, with the one on the right made from an old worn mold; mug made in two sizes;

(FIG. 194) Fenton #1040 PERSIAN MEDALLION 2-handled bon-bon, circa 1911;

(FIG. 195) CHRYSANTHEMUM pattern 9" bowl, circa 1914;

(FIG. 196) Fenton #1406 ORANGE TREE 8" bowl, with BEARDED BERRY exterior pattern, circa 1911;

(FIG. 197) Fenton #1656 DRAGON AND LOTUS 9" bowl, circa 1920.

198
Birds & Cherries
(9" Bowl)

199
Stag & Holly

200
Little Fishes
(9" Bowl)

201
Horse Medallion

202
Panther

203
Horse Medallion

204
Birds & Cherries

205
Peacock & Urn

206
Peacock & Urn
(Fenton?)

(FIG. 198) Often attributed to Northwood, BIRDS & CHERRIES is more likely Fenton—shown here in a cobalt blue 9" bowl;

(FIG. 199) Blue #1608 STAG & HOLLY bowl;

(FIG. 200) Fenton #1607 LITTLE FISHES 9" bowl in cobalt blue, circa 1921;

(FIG. 201) Fenton #1665 HORSE MEDALLION footed bon-bon in unusual aqua blue glass with marigold iridescence, circa 1912;

(FIG. 202) Fenton #1125 cobalt blue PANTHER bowl, with BUTTERFLY & BERRY exterior, circa 1914;

(FIG. 203) Fenton #1665 HORSE MEDALLION bon-bon in cobalt blue;

(FIG. 204) Fenton #1075 BIRDS & CHERRIES 2-handled bon-bon in amethyst, circa 1911;

(FIG. 205) Fenton #6 comport in PEACOCK & URN, aqua blue with marigold iridescence, circa 1912;

(FIG. 206) THIS MAY NOT BE FENTON GLASS—An expert on Millersburg carnival informed us it was probably made by John Fenton's company at Millersburg (see notes page 60).

207
Ten Mums

208
Two Flowers

209
Little Flowers

210
Plaid

211
Fenton Thistle
("Waterlily & Cattail" Exterior)

212
Concord

213
Strawberry

214
Water Lily

215
Carnival Holly

216
Pine Cone

(FIG. 207) Fenton #1057 TEN MUMS 10" bowl, blue carnival, circa 1911;

(FIG. 208) Fenton #1708 TWO FLOWERS 11" 3-footed bowl, in cobalt blue, circa 1915;

(FIG. 209) Fenton #427 LITTLE FLOWERS 10" bowl in unusual color of marigold amberina, appeared in 1910 Butler Brothers catalogue;

(FIG. 210) PLAID pattern 8½" bowl in blue—appeared in 1925 B.B. catalogue;

(FIG. 211) Fenton #1120 centerpiece bowl known as FENTON THISTLE (do not confuse for CARNIVAL THISTLE), with exterior variant pattern of WATERLILY & CATTAILS, in blue carnival, circa 1911;

(FIG. 212) Fenton #1036 CONCORD amethyst bowl with distinctive candy-ribbon edge, circa 1911;

(FIG. 213) Fenton #74 STRAWBERRY 5" bon-bon in blue, circa 1917;

(FIG. 214) Fenton #1807 WATER LILY 6" footed bon-bon in rare amber carnival;

(FIG. 215) Fenton #508 CARNIVAL HOLLY 6½" blue nappy, circa 1911;

(FIG. 216) Fenton #1064 PINE CONE 6¼" amethyst plate, circa 1911.

Novelties

217
Vintage

218
Vintage

219
Vintage

220
Grape & Cable

221
Grape & Cable

222
Vintage

223
Feathered Serpent

224
Feathered Serpent

225
Ribbon Tie

(FIG. 217) Fenton #922 VINTAGE pattern fernery, in amethyst, circa 1910;

(FIG. 218) Fenton #467 VINTAGE pattern 10" bowl, in blue, circa 1911;

(FIG. 219) VINTAGE pattern compote—note the base, stem and ruffled edge are identical to Figure 300;

(FIG. 220) Fenton's #1946 spade-footed version of the GRAPE AND CABLE pattern (also made by Northwood—see page 59). Note one cluster of the five rows of grapes at the top;

(FIG. 221) Blue Fenton #935 GRAPE AND CABLE bowl without feet, with all clusters showing only 4 rows of grapes at top (see page 59);

(FIG. 222) Fenton #466 VINTAGE pattern 8" amethyst bowl, circa 1910;

(FIG. 223) Fenton #437 FEATHERED SERPENT 9" amethyst ruffled bowl, which appeared in a 1910 B.B. catalogue;

(FIG. 224) Fenton #437 FEATHERED SERPENT blue 5½" nappy, with HONEYCOMB & CLOVER exterior pattern, circa 1910;

(FIG. 225) Blue RIBBON TIE 9" bowl, circa 1911.

Novelties

226
ackberry Banded

227
Fenton's Basket

228
Butterflies

229
Garland

230
Rustic

231
Persian Medallion

232
Leaf Chain

233
Captive Rose

234
Sailboats

235
Lions

236
Birds & Cherries

237
Leaf Chain

(FIG. 226) Blue BLACKBERRY BANDED hat-shaped novelty, circa 1912;

(FIG. 227) #1091 FENTON BASKET oval dish in blue, circa 1922;

(FIG. 228) Blue BUTTERFLIES 7" handled bon-bon, circa 1910;

(FIG. 229) Fenton #525 GARLAND 3-footed rose bowl in blue, circa 1911;

(FIG. 230) Fenton #410 7" blue RUSTIC vase, circa 1911 (similar to "April Showers", Figure 288);

(FIG. 231) Fenton #1044 PERSIAN MEDALLION 9" blue plate, circa 1911;

(FIG. 232) Fenton #1405 Blue LEAF CHAIN 8" plate, circa 1921;

(FIG. 233) Blue CAPTIVE ROSE 9" plate, year unknown; attribution is purely speculative;

(FIG. 234) Fenton #1774 SAILBOATS 5" blue nappy, circa 1914;

(FIG. 235) Blue LIONS nappy, circa 1912, also made in custard;

(FIG. 236) Cobalt blue BIRDS & CHERRIES compote, year unknown;

(FIG. 237) Fenton #1416 LEAF CHAIN 8" berry dish in blue, circa 1921—note the BEARDED BERRY exterior pattern.

238
Grape & Cable

239
Vintage

240
Birds & Cherries

241
Acorn

242
Wreath of Roses

243
Grape & Cable
("Persian Medallion" Interior)

244
Ribbon Tie

245
Fenton's Basket
("Blackberry" Interior)

246
Little Flowers
(Berry Set)

247

248
Lotus & Grape
(Variant)

(FIG. 238) Fenton #1746 GRAPE & CABLE 8" three-toed bowl, circa 1921;

(FIG. 239) Fenton #467 VINTAGE 7" nappy, which appeared in 1910 B.B. catalogue;

(FIG. 240) Fenton #1075 BIRDS & CHERRIES 6" handled bonbon, circa 1911;

(FIG. 241) Fenton #835 ACORN 7" nappy, circa 1924;

(FIG. 242) WREATH OF ROSES 5" handled bon-bon, which appeared in 1910 B.B. catalogue;

(FIG. 243) Fenton #920 GRAPE & CABLE orange bowl, circa 1911, with PERSIAN MEDALLION interior—this same bowl can be found with a plain interior. A rare find would be one with these words embossed inside, "COMPLIMENTS OF PACIFIC COAST MAIL ORDER HOUSE—LOS ANGELES";

(FIG. 244) RIBBON TIE 9" crimped bowl, circa 1911;

(FIG. 245) #1192 FENTON BASKET nut bowl with BLACKBERRY SPRAY interior, circa 1911;

(FIG. 246-247) Fenton #427 LITTLE FLOWERS berry bowl and sauce, the pattern appearing in a 1910 B.B. catalogue;

(FIG. 248) This is a variant of the LOTUS AND GRAPE pattern shown in Hartung Book 2. Attribution is speculative, but I feel certain this is Fenton.

249 (Compote)   **250** (Goblet)   **251** (Wine)

Sailboats

252

Stream of Hearts
("Persian Medallion" Ext.)

253

Illusion

254

Dragon & Berry

255

Peacock & Grapes

256

Carnival Thistle

257

Lions

258

Chrysanthemum

259

Peacock & Dahlia

(FIG. 249-251) Fenton #1802 SAILBOATS pattern compote, goblet and wine, circa 1914;

(FIG. 252) STREAM OF HEARTS ruffle-edge compote with PERSIAN MEDALLION exterior, circa 1915;

(FIG. 253) ILLUSION pattern 7" 2-handled bon-bon, date unknown;

(FIG. 254) DRAGON AND BERRY 9½" three-toed bowl, year unknown;

(FIG. 255) Fenton #1646 PEACOCK & GRAPES bowl, circa 1915;

(FIG. 256) CARNIVAL THISTLE pattern 9" bowl, circa 1911;

(FIG. 257) LIONS (STALKING LION) 8" plate with BERRY & LEAF CIRCLE exterior pattern showing through, circa 1912;

(FIG. 258) CHRYSANTHEMUM pattern 11" three-toed bowl, circa 1914;

(FIG. 259) Fenton #1645 PEACOCK & DAHLIA 7" nappy, also made in custard (see page 85), circa 1912.

Marigold Carnival

260
Heart & Horseshoe

261
Daisy Cut Bell

262
Carnival Holly

263
Peacock Tail

264
Blackberry Bramble

265
Cherry Circles

266
Pond Lily

267
April Showers
("Peacock Tail" Interior)

268
Wreath of Roses

(FIG. 260) HEART & HORSESHOE 9" bowl, year unknown;

(FIG. 261) Fenton #47 DAISY CUT BELL, called a "tea bell" in 1914 catalogue;

(FIG. 262) Fenton #208 CARNIVAL HOLLY 9½" plate, circa 1911;

(FIG. 263) PEACOCK TAIL 2-handled compote, Fenton #409 (see pg. 83);

(FIG. 264) Fenton #303 BLACKBERRY BRAMBLE compote, circa 1910;

(FIG. 265) Fenton #1426 CHERRY CIRCLES nut dish, circa 1921;

(FIG. 266) Fenton #1414 POND LILY 2-handled bon-bon, circa 1911;

(FIG. 267) Fenton #412 APRIL SHOWERS vase (this one was not stretched out) with PEACOCK TAIL interior—see also Figure 288. This pattern is very similar to Northwood's "Tree Trunk" vases;

(FIG. 268) WREATH OF ROSES 5" bon-bon, which appeared in a 1910 B.B. catalogue.

Small Items

(Photographed Close-up)

269
Vintage

270
Peacock Tail

271
Cherry Chain

272
273
Kittens

274
Peacock Tail

275
Water Lily

Swan Novelties

276
(Fenton)

277
(Northwood-Dugan)

278
(Northwood-Dugan)

(FIG. 269) Fenton #469 VINTAGE pattern tiny epergne. two pieces fitting together. circa 1911;

(FIG. 270) PEACOCK TAIL compote in blue, circa 1910;

(FIG. 271) CHERRY CHAIN 6" blue nappy. year unknown;

(FIG. 272) Cobalt blue #299 KITTENS miniature banana bowl, circa 1918;

(FIG. 273) Fenton #299 KITTENS toy-size cup in marigold, circa 1918;

(FIG. 274) Small 5" bowl in blue PEACOCK TAIL, circa 1910;

(FIG. 275) Fenton #1804 WATER LILY blue 5" crimped berry, circa 1915;

(FIG. 276-278) The SWAN NOVELTIES were made by several different companies including Fenton, Northwood, Dugan and Imperial. The Northwood and Dugan SWANS were from the same mold, and cannot be told apart today. Figures 277 and 278 are Northwood-Dugan swans. The Fenton SWAN (Figure 276) is differentiated by the distance from where the neck joins the feathered body to the position where the neck is first attached to the top of the wings. This should measure about ½ inch, whereas the Northwood measures 1¼ inches. Fenton acquired the Northwood mold in 1926 and made the swans in "Velva Rose" (see page 109).

Souvenirs & Advertising Items

279
Parkersburg Elk

280
Elk Bell

281
Atlantic City Elk

282
Soldiers & Sailors

283
Peacock Tail

284
Fenton's Basket

(FIG. 279) PARKERSBURG ELK blue 7½" plate, circa 1914.

(FIG. 280) ELK BELL, Atlantic City, in blue, circa 1911.

(FIG. 281) ATLANTIC CITY ELK 7" nappy in blue, circa 1911.

(FIG. 282) SOLDIERS & SAILORS commemorative 7½" plate in blue, with BERRY & LEAF CIRCLE exterior pattern, year unknown.

(FIG. 283) PEACOCK TAIL, Fenton #411 Violet vase, souvenir of "GENERAL FURNITURE CO., 1910".

(FIG. 284) FENTON BASKET, Fenton #1091, advertising "MILLER'S FURNITURE, 7 N. MARKET, HARRISBURG, PA., 1911", all printed on the inside base.

Late Note: Due to some careful digging into old journals, James Measell discovered how many items were produced in Atlantic City souvenirs. About 5,280 plates (bowls) and 3,840 bells were ordered. A trade journal for 1910 noted "(Fenton) has closed a contract with the Woolworth five and ten cent stores for more than 440 dozen plates with Elks heads on them and 320 dozen bells with similar design. It is stated that these souvenirs will be sold at the Grand Lodge meeting of the Elks . . . in Atlantic City."

Miscellaneous

Fentonia

285

286

Rustic Vase   *April Showers*

287   288   289   290

Zig-Zag
(Tumbler & Pitcher)

201   292

Sailboats

293   294

Peacock Tail
(Breakfast Sugar & Creamer)

295

Fentonia Fruit

296

Hearts & Trees
("Butterfly & Berry" Ext.)

297

Cherry Chain

(FIGS. 285-286) FENTONIA blue pitcher and tumbler, often confused for FENTONIA FRUIT; there is no such pattern as FENTONIA, VARIANT—the only difference between the two is one was made from an old worn mold. See also page 36;

(FIG. 287) Fenton #507 RUSTIC 16" swung vase, circa 1911;

(FIG. 288) Fenton #412 APRIL SHOWERS 10" amethyst swung vase—see also Figure 267;

(FIG. 289-290) Fenton #1015 marigold ZIG-ZAG decorated with morning glories, circa 1910;

(FIG. 291-292) Fenton #1802 SAILBOATS goblet and wine in rare blue, circa 1914;

(FIG. 293-294) PEACOCK TAIL breakfast sugar and creamer, amethyst;

(FIG. 295) FENTONIA FRUIT, Fenton's #1134 pattern, which is also known as "Cherry and Scale"—shown here in a rarely seen piece of blue (1925 B.B. catalogue);

(FIG. 296) HEARTS AND TREES interior pattern found on some BUTTERFLY & BERRY bowls, year unknown;

(FIG. 297) CHERRY CHAIN blue bowl with ORANGE TREE exterior pattern.

Miscellaneous

298 **299**
Orange Tree & Scroll

300
Iris
(compote)

301
Iris
(buttermilk goblet)

302
Orange Tr
(sundae)

303
Feather Stitch

304
Fenton Flowers

305
Cosmos Variant

306

307
Orange Tree
(Berry Set)

308
Blackberry
("Fenton Basket" Exterior)

309
Two Fruits

(FIGS. 298-299) There is no absolute proof that ORANGE TREE & SCROLL is Fenton. However, the shape, color, iridescence, and pattern design overwhelmingly lean towards Fenton as it's manufacturer. Made only in a water set, shown here in cobalt blue; Butler Bros. ads date this about 1914;

(FIG. 300-301) The IRIS compote and buttermilk goblet shown here have long been attributed to Millersburg—however. I strongly believe this is Fenton. The Butler Brothers grouping shown on page 116 seems to corroborate my theory. Also, the clear stem on the goblet is typically Fenton in nature;

(FIG. 302) ORANGE TREE pattern sherbert with clear stem and marigold bowl;

(FIG. 303) FEATHER STITCH has been attributed to Fenton by Hartung, and I am inclined to agree with her. The pattern is a more detailed and intricate variation of the COIN DOT bowl. Perhaps the same re-tooled mold was used for both.

(FIG. 304) Here is a flared dish in the #1401 FENTON FLOWERS pattern (see Figure 86), in green;

(FIG. 305) The COSMOS, VARIANT has all the characteristics of Fenton glass, but attribution here is purely speculative;

(FIG. 306-307) Master berry bowl and individual berry in ORANGE TREE pattern;

(FIG. 308) Fenton's BLACKBERRY pattern with FENTON BAS-KET exterior in red carnival;

(FIG. 309) Fenton's #1695 TWO FRUITS divided bon-bon or relish dish in blue, circa 1912.

Northwood or Fenton?

(Top Row)   *(Bottom Row)*

| 310 | 311 | 312 |
| 9½" Bowl | 8" Bowl | 7½" Bowl |

Stippled Rays   *Peacock Tail*   *Grape & Cable*

| 313 | 314 | 315 |
| Handled Bon-bon | 8" Bowl | 7" Bowl |

Illustrated above are three patterns which were made both by Fenton and by Northwood. They are shown together here for easy comparison. Usually, but not always, the Northwood version of these patterns is trademarked.

(FIGURES 310 & 313) The Fenton version of this pattern has unfortunately been incorrectly attributed to Imperial. However, the Fenton catalogue proves it was their #212 2-handled bon bon, circa 1908, shown here in amethyst. See also page 83 and 119 for various other shapes without handles. The Northwood bowl has a distinctive button in the center.

(FIGURES 311 & 314) These two bowls are most decidedly similar, but there are enough differences to tell them apart. In fact, the Northwood version of this design is known as "Nippon". Hartung reports that the pattern was made by Imperial Glass Company in 1910, appearing in their catalogue that year. It ap-

pears in Fenton's 1911 catalogue as their #407 pattern (see page 83). We have a mystery on our hands with this one.

(FIGURES 312 & 315) There are a couple of simple ways to tell Northwood's from Fenton's *Grape & Cable*. If it is trademarked with the famous N-in-a-Circle, naturally it is Northwood. Both companies made footed bowls and plates—Fenton's have either their distinctive panelled ball feet (pg. 102) or, spade-like feet (pg. 118). Northwood's have spade-like feet with the *Meander* reverse pattern. However, it becomes more difficult to tell the companies apart when identifying the non-footed variation of *Grape & Cable* bowls. According to the early catalogues, the Fenton version has four grapes at the top of the cluster placed to the right. The figure 312 example has the grapes grouped to the left.

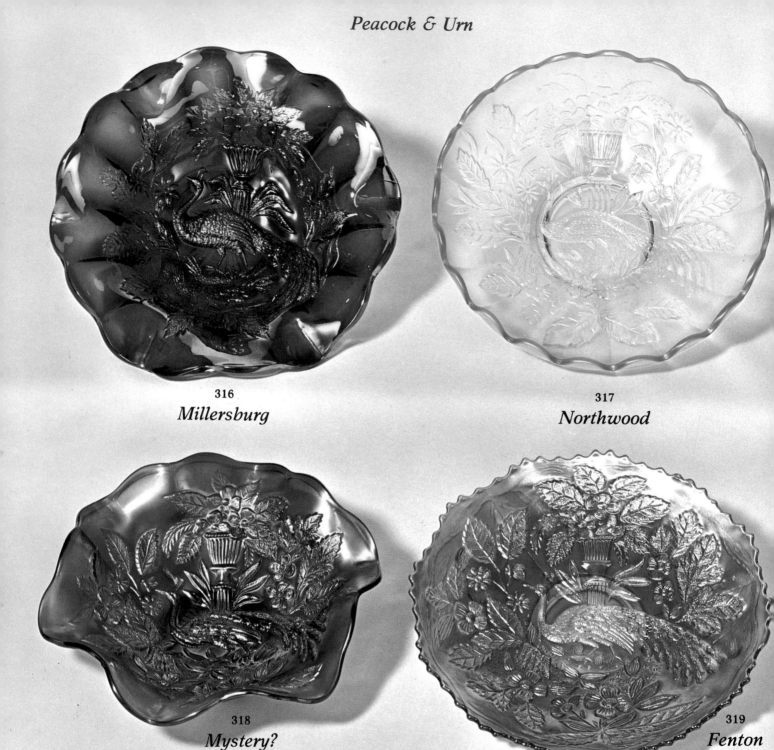

316
Millersburg

317
Northwood

318
Mystery?

319
Fenton

Other than the *Grape and Cable* bowls, and the *Little Swan* novelties, perhaps no other pattern is more difficult to attribute than *PEACOCK & URN*. However, with a little knowledge and some careful study it can become a much easier task. This pattern was made by Northwood, Millersburg **and** Fenton, so I am illustrating them all here together for comparison.

Since I am not an expert in the carnival glass field, I will list the guidelines presented by Mrs. Hartung (Book 7) on how to tell who made which. The simplest way to tell Northwood is check for the trademark. Most are marked, but unfortunately not all of them. The simplest way to denote a Fenton example is the check for a Fenton back pattern, either *Bearded Berry* or *Orange Tree*. Other than these guidelines, attribution becomes a matter of studying the pattern detail.

FIGURE 316 is a Millersburg example. It has their typical metallic lustre. Also, you will note there is no tiny bee on this piece. If the bee is missing, it is Millersburg. However, if a bee *is* present, it does not necessarily mean it is not Millersburg. Hartung states that the columned urn behind the peacock is shaped differently

from Fenton/Northwood and has no beading. There are other intricate differences which I will not attempt to go into here.

FIGURE 317 is signed Northwood in ice blue carnival. It has a panelled underside, just like Millersburg, but the urn is beaded here. On Northwood pieces, the bee is very small and almost touches the beak of the bird. There are three rows of beading on Northwood's urn, whereas there are only two on Fenton's.

FIGURE 319 is without doubt a Fenton piece. It has a *Bearded Berry* back pattern and the typical large bee, as well as other corroborative features. However, the **FIGURE 318** example is a mystery. It has characteristics of all three companies. This example was included in the Fenton Museum as one of their pieces, and I agreed with their conclusion, photographing it in a grouping of bird and animal dishes (see page 48). It does have typical Fenton color and iridescence, and the two rows of beads on the urn. However, an expert on Millersburg tells us it is not Fenton—at least not the Williamstown version of Fenton. He is certain it is Millersburg. I will let the readers decide on this one, since it is an entirely different mold from the other three examples shown here. Who do you think made it?

(FIG. 320) Fenton #888—10" vase in rare iridescent cobalt blue, circa 1925;

(FIG. 321) Fenton #200 pitcher to two-piece guest set in rare tangerine color, circa 1925;

(FIG. 322) Fenton #9—¾ lb. candy jar in rare ruby stretch glass, circa 1924;

(FIG. 323) Possibly Fenton #109 cup and plate in Wisteria stretch, circa 1921;

(FIG. 324) Fenton #1502 Celeste Blue cup in Diamond Optic, circa 1927;

(FIG. 325) Fenton "Arched Flute" (incorrectly attributed to Northwood in my second book on toothpick holders), circa 1922—the mold drawing in the Fenton archives called this a pen holder;

(FIG. 326) #66 Handled Lemon Slice Server—topaz, iridescent, circa 1926;

(FIG. 327) Possibly this is the Fenton #604 punch cup which went to the bowls illustrated on page 89, circa 1921;

328
10½" Candlestick

329
10" Candlestick

330
12" Vase

331
8½" Candlestick

332
10" Shallow Bowl

333
10" Cupped Bowl

334
6½" Flared Vase

335
7" Shallow Nappy

336
Cologne

337
Open Sugar

338
Creamer

339
11" Flared Cupped Bowl

340

341

5-Piece Ash Tray Set

(FIG. 328) Fenton #349 Wisteria 10½" candlestick, circa 1922;

(FIG. 329) Fenton #649 combination of Wisteria and Persian Pearl 10" candlestick, circa 1923;

(FIG. 330) Fenton #251 Wisteria 12" vase, circa 1922;

(FIG. 331) Fenton #449 cut Celeste Blue 8½" candlestick, circa 1923;

(FIG. 332) Fenton #601 Celeste Blue cut 10" shallow bowl, circa 1923;

(FIG. 333) Fenton #604 Wisteria 10" cupped bowl, circa 1921;

(FIG. 334) Fenton #612 Wisteria 6½" flared vase, circa 1925;

(FIG. 335) Fenton #847 shallow nappy in Wisteria, circa 1926;

(FIG. 336) Fenton #55 Celeste Blue cologne, circa 1924;

(FIG. 337-338) Fenton #2 creamer and open sugar in Celeste Blue with Royal Blue handles, circa 1924;

(FIG. 339) This could possibly be Fenton's #647 flared cupped bowl, almost 11" in diameter, in a rare amber color, circa 1921;

(FIG. 340-341) Fenton #202 Celeste Blue 5-piece ash tray set, circa 1923.

Stretch Glass
Tangerine & Grecian Gold

342
16" Vase

343
10" Bud Vase

344
Candy Jar

345
8" Fan Vase

346
Candlestick

347
Oval Butter Tray

348
8" Cupped Bowl

349
11" Flared Bowl

350
High-Standard Compote

351
Rose Bowl

352
10" 2-Tone Candlestick

353
Powder Puff

(FIG. 342) Fenton #1531 Tangerine 16" vase, circa 1927;

(FIG. 343) Fenton #251, 10" bud vase in Tangerine color, circa 1927;

(FIG. 344) Fenton #835 Tangerine candy jar, circa 1926;

(FIG. 345) Fenton #857, 8" Fan vase in Tangerine, circa 1927;

(FIG. 346) Fenton #316 Tangerine candlestick, circa 1927;

(FIG. 347) Fenton #318 handled oval butter tray in Tangerine, circa 1925;

(FIG. 348) Fenton #857 Tangerine 8" cupped bowl, circa 1925;

(FIG. 349) Fenton #857, 11" flared bowl in Tangerine, circa 1927;

(FIG. 350) This high-standard compote, originally called a footed bowl, appears in a Fenton catalogue without a number assigned. The color is Grecian Gold, and it dates about 1925;

(FIG. 351) Fenton #847 Grecian Gold rose bowl, circa 1927;

(FIG. 352) Fenton #649, 10" candlestick, two-tone Grecian Gold and Black, circa 1923;

(FIG. 353) Fenton #57 Grecian Gold powder puff, circa 1925.

354
Flared Cupped Comport

355
6" Candlestick

356
Crimped Orange Bowl

357
8" Fan Vase

358
Night Set

359
7½" Flared Bowl

360
10" Handled Oval Tray

361
7" Butter Ball

362
Footed Fern Dish

363
Covered Bon-bon

364
Covered Puff Box

365
Cologne

366
5" Lily Bowl

(FIG. 354) Fenton #738 flared cupped comport, circa 1924;

(FIG. 355) Fenton #249, 6" candlestick, circa 1921;

(FIG. 356) Fenton #603 10" crimped orange bowl, circa 1921;

(FIG. 357) Fenton #572, 8" Fan vase, circa 1926;

(FIG. 358) Fenton #401 night set, circa 1922;

(FIG. 359) Fenton #847, 7½" flared bowl, circa 1926;

(FIG. 360) Fenton #1561, 10" oval handled tray, circa 1926;

(FIG. 361) Fenton #318, 7" Butter ball, circa 1925;

(FIG. 362) Fenton #250 footed fern dish, circa 1921;

(FIG. 363) This appears to be Fenton's #643 covered bon-bon, with the stenciled inscription "60th Anniversary—Schiller Lodge No. 345—F & AM—June 10, 1924";

(FIG. 364) Fenton #743 covered puff box, circa 1924;

(FIG. 365) Fenton #56 cologne with drip stopper, circa 1925;

(FIG. 366) Fenton #575, 5" lily bowl, circa 1924.

367
12" Swung Vase

368
12" Bud Vase

369
Guest Set

370
½ lb. Candy Jar

371
1 lb. Candy Jar

372
5¼" Fan Vase

373
10" Crimped Bowl

374
Dolphin Candlestick

375
Candlestick

376
Candlestick

377
Nut Cup

378
Mayonnaise & Ladle

379
½ lb. Candy Jar

380
Cologne

(FIG. 367) Fenton #574, 12" swung vase with crimped top, circa 1926;

(FIG. 368) Fenton #251, 12" bud vase, circa 1926;

(FIG. 369) Fenton #200 Guest set, circa 1926;

(FIG. 370) Fenton #835, ½ lb. candy jar, circa 1926;

(FIG. 371) Fenton #636, 1 lb. candy jar, circa 1926;

(FIG. 372) Fenton #1533, 5¼" dolphin-handled fan vase, circa 1927;

(FIG. 373) Fenton #1504A, 10" crimped bowl with dolphins, circa 1928;

(FIG. 374) Fenton #1623 dolphin candlestick, circa 1928;

(FIG. 375) Fenton #318 candlestick, circa 1926;

(FIG. 376) Fenton #314 candlestick, circa 1926;

(FIG. 377) Fenton #923 individual nut dish, circa 1926;

(FIG. 378) Fenton #923 mayonnaise and ladle, circa 1926;

(FIG. 379) Fenton #568, ½ lb. candy jar with cover, circa 1926;

(FIG. 380) Fenton #59 cologne, circa 1926;

381
Fenton #636
(candy jar)

382
Northwood #636
(candy jar)

383
Fenton #349
10" Candlestick

384
Northwood #696
10" Candlestick

385
8½" Candle

386
Crimped Bon-Bon

387
Covered Puff Jar

388
Fern Bowl

389
Nut Cup

390
½ lb. Candy Jar

391
Sandwich Tray

392
Puff Jar

393
9" Cupped Bowl

(FIG. 381) Fenton #636, 1 lb. candy jar, circa 1921;

(FIG. 382) This is the almost identical Northwood #636 candy jar. The difference between the two is that the mold line runs along the left side of the ribs on Fenton's and along the right side of the ribs on Northwood's. Circa 1924;

(FIG. 383) Fenton #349, 10" candlestick, circa 1921;

(FIG. 384) Northwood #696, 10" candlestick, with only slight mold variations, circa 1924;

(FIG. 385) Fenton #549, 8½" candlestick, circa 1923;

(FIG. 386) Fenton #574 crimped flared bon-bon, circa 1926;

(FIG. 387) Fenton #53 covered puff jar, circa 1926;

(FIG. 388) Fenton #250 fern bowl, circa 1921;

(FIG. 389) Fenton #923 individual nut cup, circa 1925;

(FIG. 390) Fenton #735, ½ lb. candy jar, circa 1925;

(FIG. 391) Fenton #317 sandwich tray, circa 1924;

(FIG. 392) Fenton #53 covered puff jar, circa 1926;

(FIG. 393) Fenton #604, 9" cupped bowl, circa 1921.

394
Candy Bowl

395
Candlestick

396
Bud Vase

397
11" Flared Bowl

398
Grape Juice Pitcher

399
5" Etched Fan Vase

400
8" Salad Plate

401
Candlestick

402
Dolphin Fan Vase

403
Decorated Candlestick

404
Cigarette Holder

405
Trademark Sign

406
Open Sugar

407
Creamer

(FIG. 394) Fenton #844 candy bowl in Florentine Green, circa 1927;

(FIG. 395) Fenton #232 8" candlestick, circa 1925;

(FIG. 396) Fenton #354 8" bud vase, circa 1928;

(FIG. 397) Fenton #647, almost 11" flared cupped bowl, circa 1921;

(FIG. 398) Fenton #215 grape juice pitcher, circa 1921;

(FIG. 399) Fenton #570, 5" decorated Fan vase, circa 1926;

(FIG. 400) Fenton #681, 8" salad plate with decoration #2, circa 1925;

(FIG. 401) Fenton #316 candlestock, circa 1926;

(FIG. 402) Fenton #1533, 2-handled dolphin fan vase, circa 1927;

(FIG. 403) Fenton #317 decorated candlestick, circa 1927;

(FIG. 404) Fenton #554 cigarette holder, circa 1925;

(FIG. 405) Fenton Art Glass Trademark sign, from the 1920's;

(FIG. 406-407) Fenton #3 open sugar and creamer, circa 1927.

408
10½" Oval Bowl

409
Round Comport

410
5" Fan Vase
Diamond Optic

411
6" Crimped Square Bon-I
Diamond Optic

412
10" Cut Oval Bowl

413
9" Cupped Bowl

414
5" Cut Fan Vase

415
Candlestick

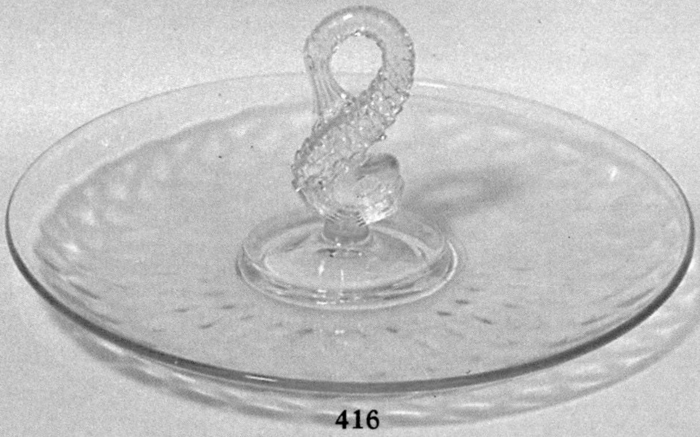

416
10" Sandwich Tray
Diamond Optic

417
8½" Cupped Bowl
Diamond Optic

(FIG. 408) Fenton #1608, 10½" deep oval bowl, in Aquamarine stretch, circa 1926;

(FIG. 409) Fenton #1533 round comport, in Tangerine, circa 1927;

(FIG. 410) Fenton #1532, 5" fan vase in Diamond Optic pattern, Orchid color, circa 1927;

(FIG. 411) Fenton #1533, 6" Diamond Optic square crimped bon-bon, Orchid color, circa 1927;

(FIG. 412) Fenton #1621-1703, 10" deep oval bowl with cut decoration, Aquamarine color, circa 1928;

(FIG. 413) Fenton #1504A, 9" cupped bowl in scarce Turquoise opaque, circa 1928;

(FIG. 414) Fenton #1532A-1702, 5" fan vase with cut decoration, Aquamarine color, circa 1928;

(FIG. 415) Fenton #1623 green candlestick, circa 1928;

(FIG. 416) Fenton #1502A, 10" sandwich tray in Diamond Optic, pale green, circa 1927;

(FIG. 417) Fenton #1502, 8½" flared cupped bowl, Aquamarine color, circa 1927.

Jade Green

418
11" Flared Bowl

419
10" Vase

420
10½" Wicker-Handle Basket

421
Candy Jar

422
10" Crimped Bowl

423
September Morn Nymph
in Flared Bowl

424

425
Console Set

426
Candlestick

427
Rolled Edge Bowl

428
Candlesticks

429
Candlestick

430
Lemon Tray

(FIG. 418) Fenton #160, 11" flared bowl with dolphins, circa 1928;

(FIG. 419) Fenton #251, 10" bud vase, circa 1922;

(FIG. 410) Fenton #1681, 10½" wicker-handled basket, circa 1931;

(FIG. 421) Fenton #1532 candy jar with dolphin handles, circa 1927;

(FIG. 422) Fenton #857, 10" crimped bowl, circa 1927;

(FIG. 423) Fenton #1645 "September Morn Nymph" standing in #857 flared bowl, circa 1928;

(FIG. 424-425) Fenton #848 or (#1234) flower-form console set (second candlestick missing), circa 1932; see page 113;

(FIG. 426) Fenton #1623 candlestick with dolphins, circa 1928;

(FIG. 427) Fenton #1504A-10 rolled-edge bowl, circa 1928;

(FIG. 428) Fenton #316 candlestick, circa 1926;

(FIG. 429) Fenton #318 candlestick, circa 1926;

(FIG. 430) Fenton #66 handled lemon tray, circa 1926.

Fenton Rose

431

432
**Iced Tea Set
Diamond Optic**

433
9 oz. Goblet

434
**Iced Tea Set
Ming Rose**

435

436
Flower Pot & Base

437
Oval Comport

438
Diamond Optic Ice Bucket

439
**7" Cupped Bowl
Diamond Optic**

440
Turtle Flower Block

441
Cut Ash Tray

442
Dolphin-Handled Plate

443
Cut Sherbert

(FIG. 431-432) Fenton #1636-1702 Diamond Optic iced tea set, circa 1928;

(FIG. 433) Fenton #1640, 9 oz. bridge goblet, with special hand cut design by James D. Fenton about 1928, part of a set which also includes Figures 441 and 443; see page 110;

(FIG. 434-435) Fenton #1653 "Ming Rose" iced tea set, circa 1934;

(FIG. 436) Fenton #1554 flower pot and base, circa 1927;

(FIG. 437) Possibly Fenton, this dolphin-stemmed oval comport does not appear in existing catalogues—circa 1929; reportedly this item is one of a kind, as it was not commercially produced.

(FIG. 438) Fenton #1616-1702 ice bucket in Diamond Optic pattern, cut decoration, circa 1928;

(FIG. 439) Fenton #1502-A Diamond Optic 7" cupped bowl, circa 1928;

(FIG. 440) Fenton #1564 Turtle flower block, circa 1927;

(FIG. 441) Ash tray to bridge set, cut by James D. Fenton, circa 1928;

(FIG. 442) Dolphin-handled plate with Fenton's #1521 cut decoration, circa 1928;

(FIG. 443) Sherbert to bridge set cut by James D. Fenton, circa 1928.

Mandarin Red

444
Mikado Comport

445
10" Candlestick

446
8" Flared Vase

447
Leaf Tiers Cupped Bowl

448
Pipe Ash Tray

449
Mikado Cake Stand

450
Shallow Cupped Bowl & Base

451
11" Flared Bowl

(FIG. 444) Fenton's #919 MIKADO pattern 10" diameter comport (originally called a "flared footed bowl" in catalogue), in Mandarin Red, known popularly today as red slag, circa 1934;

(FIG. 445) Fenton #449 8½" candlestick, circa 1924, in Venetian Red.

(FIG. 446) Fenton #621, 8" flared vase, circa 1934;

(FIG. 447) #1790, 10" cupped bowl in LEAF TIERS pattern, circa 1934;

(FIG. 448) Unusual pipe ash tray, with resting place for pipe, patent dated at base;

(FIG. 449) Fenton #919 MIKADO pattern footed cake plate, circa 1934;

(FIG. 450) Fenton #601 shallow cupped bowl with black glass base, circa 1924, in Venetian Red;

(FIG. 451) Fenton #1663, 11" flared bowl, circa 1932.

Fenton Cameo

452
13" Swung Vase

453
Flared Bowl

454
Trumpet Vase

455
8" Fan Vase

456
Candlestick

456
Candlestick

457
Candy Jar

458
Open Sugar

459
Creamer

460
Candy Jar
(lid missing)

461
Candlestick

462
Cupped Bowl

463
Cupped Bowl

(FIG. 452) Fenton #1631 Cameo line in a 13" Swung vase, circa 1927;

(FIG. 453) Fenton #1512 9" Bowl, circa 1926;

(FIG. 454) Fenton #573 Trumpet vase, circa 1927;

(FIG. 455) Fenton #857 8" Fan vase, circa 1926;

(FIG. 456) Fenton #318 candlesticks, circa 1926;

(FIG. 457) Fenton #1532 Candy Jar, circa 1929;

(FIG. 458-459) Attribution of this is based on existing mold drawings with the same design shown on this creamer and sugar. Reportedly this was made in 1916;

(FIG. 460) Fenton #736 Candy Jar (1 lb.) with lid missing, circa 1926; see lid on ad reprint, page 86;

(FIG. 461) Fenton #316 candlestick, circa 1927;

(FIG. 462) Fenton #847 cupped bowl, circa 1926;

(FIG. 463) Fenton #53 base to powder jar of a dresser set, circa 1927.

Marigold

464
8" Vase

465
¾ lb. Candy Jar

466

467
Water Set

468
Guest Set

469
8½" Candlestick

470
7" Footed Comport

471
½ lb. Candy Jar,

472
Cologne

473
Cigarette Holder

474
6" Candlestick

(FIG. 464) Fenton #3700, 8" vase, circa 1918;

(FIG. 465) Fenton #9 candy jar with #3600 grape cutting, circa 1916;

(FIG. 466-467) Fenton #3600 water set, part of "Grecian Cut Gold Assortment", circa 1916;

(FIG. 468) Fenton #200, 2-piece guest set with royal blue handle, circa 1924;

(FIG. 469) Fenton #232, 8½" candlestick, circa 1925;

(FIG. 470) Fenton #260, 7" footed comport, circa 1923;

(FIG. 471) Fenton #8, ½ lb. candy jar, circa 1921;

(FIG. 472) Fenton #56 cologne with unusual #55½ stopper, circa 1925;

(FIG. 473) Fenton #556 cigarette holder, circa 1925;

(FIG. 473) Fenton #249 candlestick, circa 1921.

Fenton Ruby
(Plain & Stretch)

475
10" Crimped Orange Bowl

476
8½" Cut Candlestick

477
Shallow Cupped Bowl

478
Fenton Basket
8" Crimped Nappy

479
Fenton Basket
7" Bon-Bon

480
Footed Sherbert

481
8" Cupped Bowl

Lincoln Inn

482
6½" Tulip Vase

483
Candlestick

484
10" Cupped Bowl

485
Finger Bowl

486
Wine

(FIG. 475) Fenton #603, 10" crimped orange bowl in rare ruby stretch glass, circa 1921;

(FIG. 476) Fenton #449, 8½" cut candlestick in ruby stretch, circa 1922;

(FIG. 477) Fenton #606 ruby stretch shallow cupped bowl, circa 1921;

(FIG. 478) Fenton #1093 FENTON BASKET 8" crimped nappy, circa 1934;

(FIG. 479) Fenton #1092, 7" bon-bon in FENTON BASKET pattern, circa 1930;

(FIG. 480) Fenton #1639 footed sherbert with clear base, circa 1930;

(FIG. 481) Fenton #231, 8" cupped bowl, circa 1929;

(FIG. 482) Fenton #107, 6½" tulip vase, circa 1933;

(FIG. 483) Fenton #1623 candlestick with dolphins, circa 1930;

(FIG. 484) Fenton #1504A, 10" cupped bowl with dolphins, circa 1930;

(FIG. 485) Fenton #1700 finger bowl in LINCOLN INN pattern, circa 1928;

(FIG. 486) Fenton #1700 wine glass in LINCOLN INN pattern, circa 1928.

487   488   489   490   491   492

493   494   495   496   497

(FIG. 487-488) Fenton #222 blue opalescent iced tea set in Rib Optic line, circa 1922;

(FIG. 489-490) Fenton #222 plain Topaz colored iced tea set with base and casters in royal blue, circa 1922;

(FIG. 491-492) Fenton #220 green opalescent iced tea set with cover, circa 1926;

(FIG. 493) Fenton #220 Celeste Blue iced tea pitcher with cover, circa 1922;

(FIG. 494) Fenton #200 Topaz 2-piece guest set, circa 1926;

(FIG. 495) Fenton #200 Persian Pearl (white stretch) 2-piece guest set, circa 1926;

(FIG. 496) Fenton #200 CURTAIN OPTIC pitcher to guest set, iridescent Topaz opalescent, circa 1926;

(FIG. 497) Fenton #222 iced tea tumbler in Wisteria iridescent cut, circa 1922.

Cherry & Scale

498
Butter

499
Tumbler

500
Pitcher

499
Tumbler

501
Spooner

502
Sugar

503
Master
Berry

504
Sauce

505
Horse
Medallions

506
Stalking
Lion

507
Lotus
& Grape

508
Persian
Medallion

(FIGS. 498-504) In my custard glass book I dated this pattern about 1908—however, we now know that CHERRY & SCALE was made about 1915. In carnival glass it is known as *Fentonia Fruit,* and is quite scarce. It seems unfortunate that a single pattern should carry two names, but this one we must live with, since carnival collectors are as enthusiastic about one name as custard collectors are about the other. This line was Fenton's #1134 pattern, and the catalogue reprint is shown on page 100. The glass is stained a nutmeg brown, and except for the creamer, all known pieces are illustrated here;

(FIG. 505) Fenton's #1665 HORSE MEDALLION bowl with "Berry & Leaf Circle" back pattern. All the custard novelties date about 1915. See page 85;

(FIG. 506) The LION or "Stalking Lion" pattern can easily be attributed to Fenton because of the pattern characteristics, the color staining shown here, and the "Berry and Leaf Circle" back pattern—also made in carnival colors;

(FIG. 507) I incorrectly called this *Dragon and Lotus* in my custard book—it is, of course, LOTUS AND GRAPE instead. Attribution is based on pattern and obvious color-staining characteristics, as we have no catalogue listings;

(FIG. 508) Fenton's #548 PERSIAN MEDALLION pattern rose bowl with green staining.

Fenton Animals

510
Elephant
Flower Bowl

509
Turtle
Flower Bowl

Few collectors are aware of the fact that Fenton also made a limited number of glass animals, which are highly popular today. Illustrated here is Fenton's #1565 Turtle flower bowl, which was also made with a lid as a covered bon-bon and as a base to a small plain crystal fish bowl. It was made about 1929, and according to the ad on page 97, in green only. It is 9" long and quite scarce.

Also shown above is a very rare #1618 Elephant flower bowl in a most unusual color of teal blue. It is also known in crystal,

light green and pale rose. It appeared in Fenton's 1929 catalogue (see page 110).

I would like to thank Mrs. Jean Cline for lending these choice examples to me for inclusion in this book. Her mother acquired these pieces directly from the factory, and Jean played with them as a child. Remarkably they are still in like-new condition.

511

512

Illustrated above are the very rare Fenton Butterfly Ornaments which were originally given away as premiums along with a larger glass purchase. We have no catalogue illustrations to verify these are Fenton (Presznick calls them "Northwood Moths"), but the few examples I know of were acquired directly from early Fenton workers or their families who swear they came directly from the factory. Also the Dec. 31, 1917 inventory of iridescent ware lists 70 dozen "butter flies". The fact that these rarities do not show up in a catalogue leads me to believe that they were not commercially produced, and indeed were given away. Mrs. Cline tells me that the butterflies were attached to the handles of glass baskets with a dab of putty. No matter what their actual purpose was, they are extremely hard to find today.

The Butterflies shown here are in white and light blue carnival glass, and date quite close to the end of this era, about 1928. They have been chosen as the official symbol of the Fenton Art Glass Collectors of America.

FENTON ART GLASS

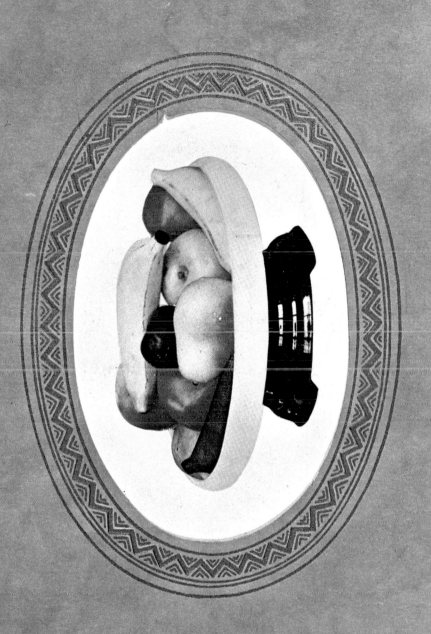

THE FENTON ART GLASS COMPANY
WILLIAMSTOWN, WEST VIRGINIA, U.S.A.

On the following pages are a number of catalogue reprints in their original color. Unfortunately, none of the catalogues before 1932 were dated. The only methods we can use to determine the approximate year or publication is to assume that the catalogue items will appear in the company inventories, in dated advertisements, in trade journal notices, or in jobber catalogues (Butler Brothers). Existing Fenton inventory records are incomplete, with some years much more extensive than others. For this reason, the dating of the catalogues reprinted in this section must be considered an "educated guess". You must also bear in mind that many popular patterns were made for several years, and often earlier molds were revived in later years for additional production.

Wide assortment of Mosaic Inlaid art glass, circa 1926.

Wide assortment of *Butterfly & Berry* pattern, circa 1911.

SPECIAL SUNSET
IRIDESCENT LEMONADE
SET ASSORTMENT.

out.

No. 1109 - VIOLET

No. 910 - GREEN

Out

No. 1012 - ROYAL

Water sets (Lemonade) in *Fluffy Peacock, Butterfly and Fern,* and *Floral and Grape Variant* patterns. The pattern above is Fenton's *Floral & Grape Variant.* It has ten petals on the daisy closest to the handle and the ribs lean to the right. The three examples photographed in this book (Figs. 138, 162, 172) have eight-petalled flowers and the ribs lean to the left. They were made by Dugan-Diamond, not Fenton. See page 118.

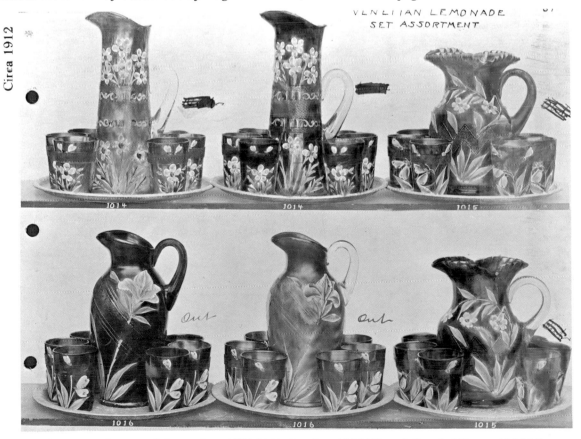

VENETIAN LEMONADE
SET ASSORTMENT

1014   1014   1015

out   *out*

1016   1016   1015

Lemonade sets in decorated *Prism Band* (#1014), *Zig-Zag* (#1015) and *Banded Drape* (#1016) patterns.

81

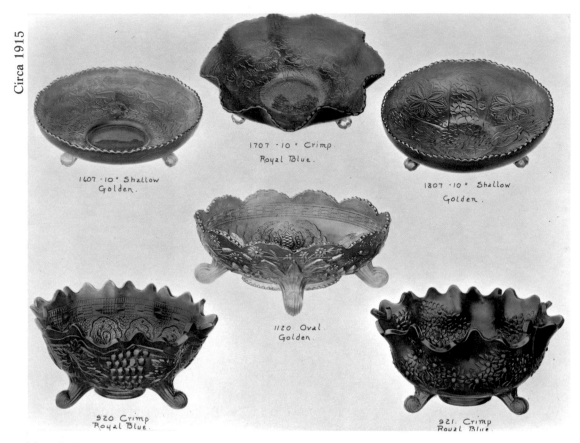

Assorted bowls in *Little Fishes* (#1607), *Two Flowers* (#1707), *Water Lily* (#1807), *Fenton Thistle* (#1120), *Grape & Cable* with *Persian Medallion* interior (#920) and *Orange Tree* (#921).

Assorted bowls and nappies in *Carnival Holly* (#208) and *Vintage* (#466).

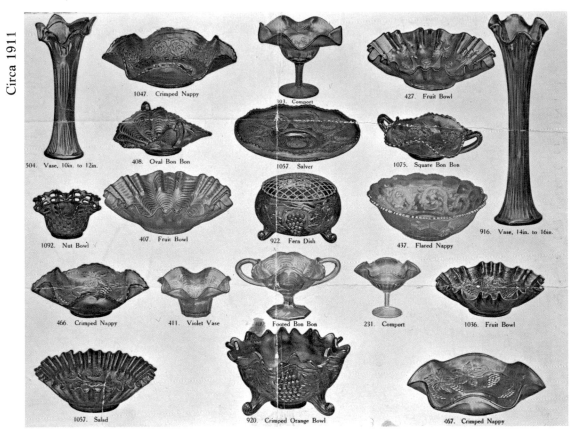

504. Vase, 10in. to 12in.	1047. Crimped Nappy	303. Comport	427. Fruit Bowl
	408. Oval Bon Bon	1057. Salver	1075. Square Bon Bon
1092. Nut Bowl	407. Fruit Bowl	922. Fern Dish	437. Flared Nappy
			916. Vase, 14in. to 16in.
466. Crimped Nappy	411. Violet Vase	409. Footed Bon Bon	231. Comport	1036. Fruit Bowl
1057. Salad	920. Crimped Orange Bowl	467. Crimped Nappy	

Wide novelty assortment, including *Diamond & Rib* (#504), *Persian Medallion* (#1047), *Blackberry Bramble* (#303), *Little Flowers* (#427), *Peacock Tail* (#407, 411, 408), *Ten Mums* (#1057), *Birds and Cherries* (#1075), *Vintage* (#922), *Feathered Serpent* (#437), *Concord* (#1036), *Vintage* nappy (#467), *Grape & Cable* with plain interior (#920), and *Rib & Holly Sprig* compote (#231).

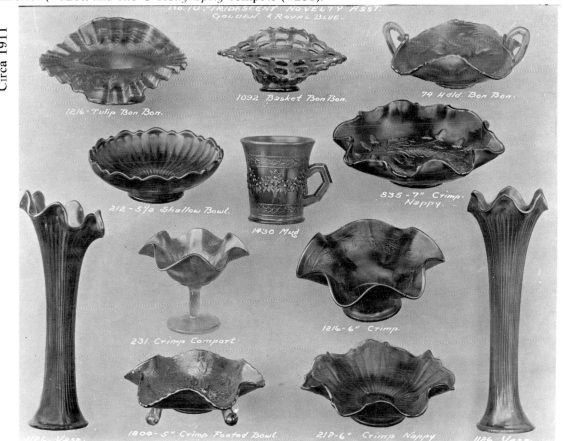

No. 10 IRIDESCENT NOVELTY ASST.
GOLDEN & ROYAL BLUE.

1216 - Tulip Bon Bon. 1092. Basket Bon Bon. 74 Hdld. Bon Bon.

212 - 5½ Shallow Bowl. 1430 Mug 835 - 7" Crimp. Nappy.

231. Crimp Comport. 1216 - 6" Crimp.

1804 - 5" Crimp Footed Bowl. 212 - 6" Crimp Nappy

1126 Vase. 1126 Vase.

Assortment of novelties; *Blackberry Spray* (#1216), *Fenton Basket* (#1092), *Strawberry* (#74), *Stippled Rays* with *Scale Band* exterior (#212), *Orange Tree* (#1430), *Acorn* (#835), *Fenton Rib* (#1126), *Carnival Holly* (#231), *Water Lily* (#1804), *Rib & Holly Sprig*.

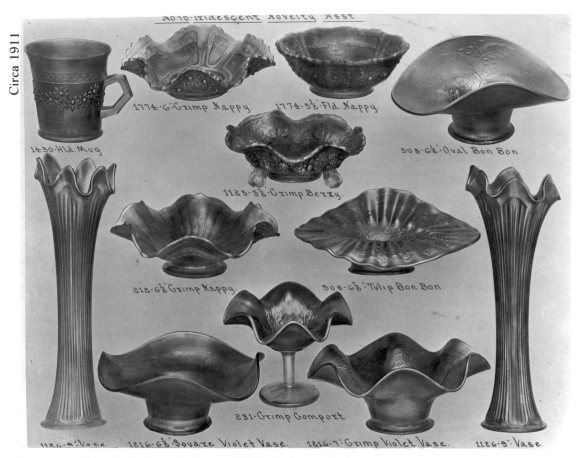

More Fenton novelties, including *Sailboats* (#1774), *Butterfly & Berry* with *Hearts & Trees* interior (#1125), *Carnival Holly* bon-bons (#508), *Fenton Rib* vases (#1126) and *Rib & Holly Sprig* compote (#231).

Wide assortment of *Orange Tree,* including #1406 grape dish, #1411 breakfast creamer & sugar, #1403 puff box, #413 loving cup, #406 cake plate and #410 hat pin holder; also #548 *Persian Medallions*, #410 *Rustic* vase, #266 *Pond Lily.*

Illustrated here is a novelty assortment in color-stained Fenton custard glass, originally called "Peach Blow" by Fenton; *Pond Lily* (#5), *Sailboats* (#7), a No. 2 *Rose Mug*, *Butterfly & Berry* vase (#1124), *Peacock & Dahlia* (#1645), *Blackberry Banded* novelties (#3, 6) and *Sailboats* compote (#1802).

Another novelty assortment in custard glass with "goofus" type decoration, including items in *Prayer Rug*, *Blackberry Banded*, the *Rose Mug*, and a #526 *Strawberry?* jelly compote (incorrectly attributed to Northwood in my *Custard Glass* book).

FENTON ART GLASS

No. 349—10-inch CANDLESTICK — Celeste Blue
No. 449—8" CANDLESTICK — Florentine Green
No. 249—6" CANDLESTICK — Grecian Gold
No. 636—1-lb. CANDY JAR — Celeste Blue
No. 8—½-lb. CANDY JAR — Grecian Gold
No. 9—¾-lb. CANDY JAR — Florentine Green
No. 736—1-lb. CANDY JAR — Topaz
No. 251—10" BUD VASE — Celeste Blue

No. 9—7" CRIMPED COMPORT — Florentine Green
No. 9—7½" OVAL COMPORT — Celeste Blue
No. 400—6" SQUARE VASE — Florentine Green
No. 400—6" CRIMPED VASE — Persian Pearl
No. 106—6½" CRIMPED BON BON — Florentine Green
No. 103 SHERBET AND PLATE — Iridescent Wistaria

No. 643 COVERED BON BON — Celeste Blue
No. 643 CUPPED BON BON — Topaz
No. 643—6¾" SALVER COMPOTE — Grecian Gold
No. 643—7" PLATE COMPOTE — Topaz
No. 250 FOOTED FERN DISH — Celeste Blue
No. 401 NIGHT SET — Grecian Gold

No. 631—9½" CAKE PLATE — Celeste Blue
No. 630—8½" SALAD PLATE — Plain Wistaria
No. 644—7¾" BAKED APPLE DISH — Celeste Blue
No. 1005 SALAD PLATE — Florentine Green
No. 301—6" PLATE — Celeste Blue
2" Flower Block
3" Flower Block

FENTON ART GLASS

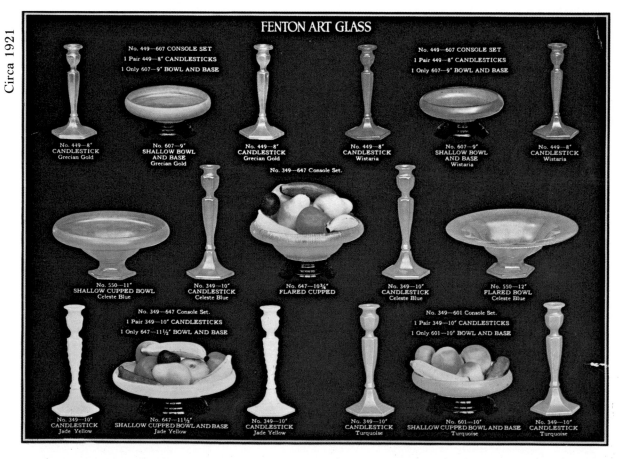

No. 449—607 CONSOLE SET
1 Pair 449—8" CANDLESTICKS
1 Only 607—9" BOWL AND BASE

No. 449—607 CONSOLE SET
1 Pair 449—8" CANDLESTICKS
1 Only 607—9" BOWL AND BASE

No. 449—8" CANDLESTICK — Grecian Gold
No. 607—9" SHALLOW BOWL AND BASE — Grecian Gold
No. 449—8" CANDLESTICK — Grecian Gold
No. 449—8" CANDLESTICK — Wistaria
No. 607—9" SHALLOW BOWL AND BASE — Wistaria
No. 449—8" CANDLESTICK — Wistaria

No. 349—647 Console Set.

No. 550—11" SHALLOW CUPPED BOWL — Celeste Blue
No. 349—10" CANDLESTICK — Celeste Blue
No. 647—10¾" FLARED CUPPED
No. 349—10" CANDLESTICK — Celeste Blue
No. 550—12" FLARED BOWL — Celeste Blue

No. 349—647 Console Set.
1 Pair 349—10" CANDLESTICKS
1 Only 647—11½" BOWL AND BASE

No. 349—601 Console Set.
1 Pair 349—10" CANDLESTICKS
1 Only 601—10" BOWL AND BASE

No. 349—10" CANDLESTICK — Jade Yellow
No. 647—11½" SHALLOW CUPPED BOWL AND BASE — Jade Yellow
No. 349—10" CANDLESTICK — Jade Yellow
No. 349—10" CANDLESTICK — Turquoise
No. 601—10" SHALLOW CUPPED BOWL AND BASE — Turquoise
No. 349—10" CANDLESTICK — Turquoise

Wide assortment of items in Fenton stretch, listed by number, item definition and color—note the spelling of Wisteria. Every item shown on pages 86 & 87 may be found in any of the 12 colors.

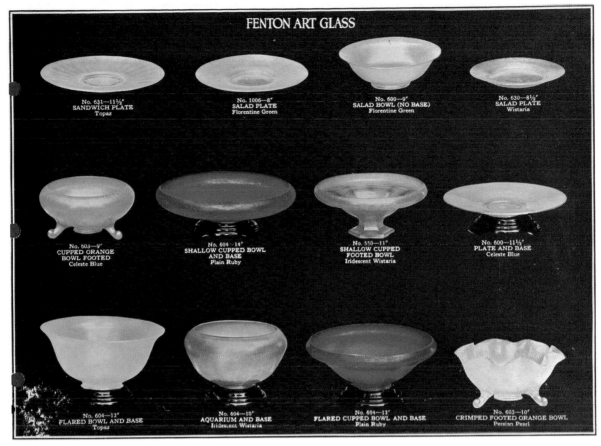

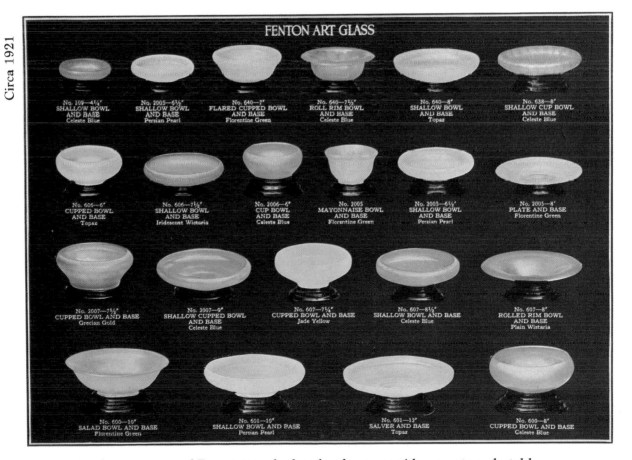

Wide assortment of Fenton stretch glass bowls, some with separate pedestal bases.

Assortment of Fenton stretch glass—note the listing of the jet black "Ebony" line which is apparently very rare today.

Assortment of Fenton's Tangerine colored stretch glass.

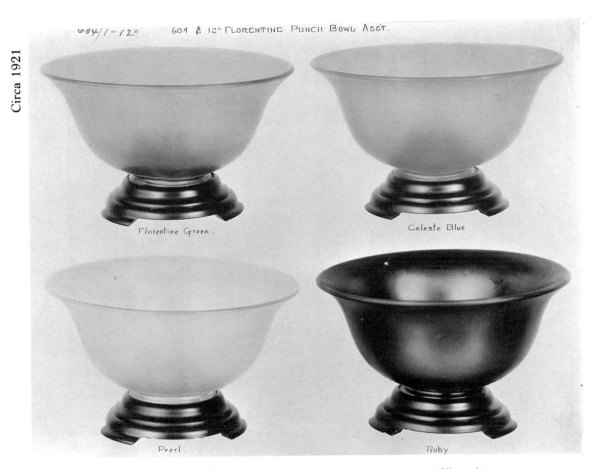

Assortment of colors in #604 punch bowls, which are only 12" in diameter.

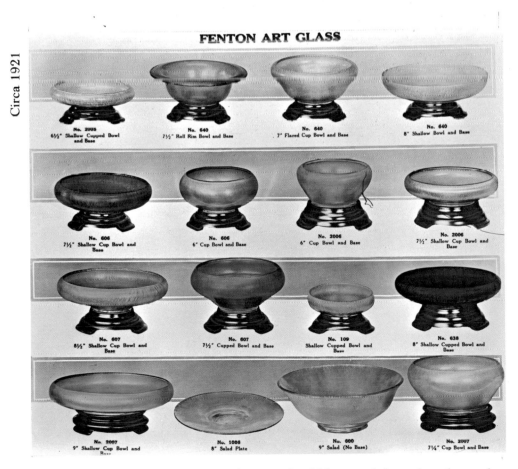

Assortment of bowls and plates in Fenton stretch glass—it should be noted that other glassmakers made these bowls in almost identical shapes and sizes.

32 PIECE FENTON FLORENTINE ASST 1925.   68118.

847-8"   640-7"   231-10"   643

449-8½"   449-8½"   550-12"   643-6¾"   891-12"   612-6½"

550-12½"   232-8½"   846-8¾"   232-8½"   735-½

More items in Fenton stretch glass, dated 1925.

ELITE ASSORTMENT   22624·C

103 · 6 Pieces
G. Gold
Sherbet & Plate

643/5 ·Covered BonBon
Plain Ruby

643/5 ·Covered BonBon
G. Gold

643/5 ·Covered BonBon
C. Blue

220/222
Plain Topaz
Ice Tea Set

736/6½ ·Comport
Plain Ruby

222/222
Iridescent Topaz
Lemonade Set

602 -10" Vase & Base
G. Gold

736/6½ ·Comport
C. Blue

602 -10" Vase & Base
C. Blue

736/6½ ·Comport
G. Gold

602 -10" Vase & Base
Plain Ruby

Assortment of pitchers, vases, etc. in Fenton stretch glass.

Many additional items in various colors of Fenton stretch glass.

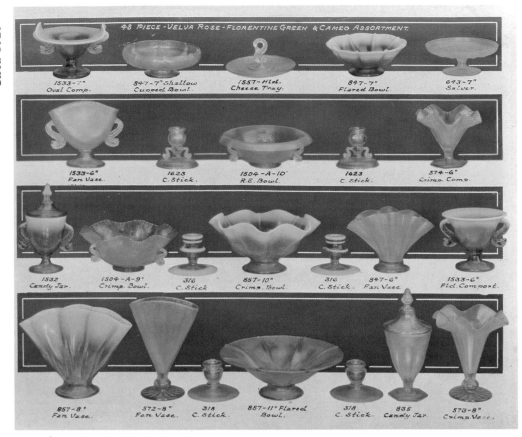

Assortment of items in Cameo colored glass and others in Fenton stretch.

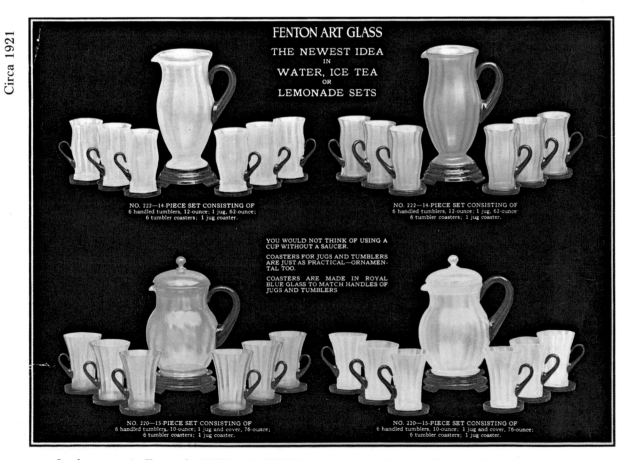

Iced tea sets in Fenton's #220 and #222 line, complete with handled tumblers and coasters.

Several more items in Fenton's stretch glass, all numbered and identified.

Assortment of items in colors of aquamarine, rose and green.

Complete set of *Banded Laurel* pattern made in persian blue.

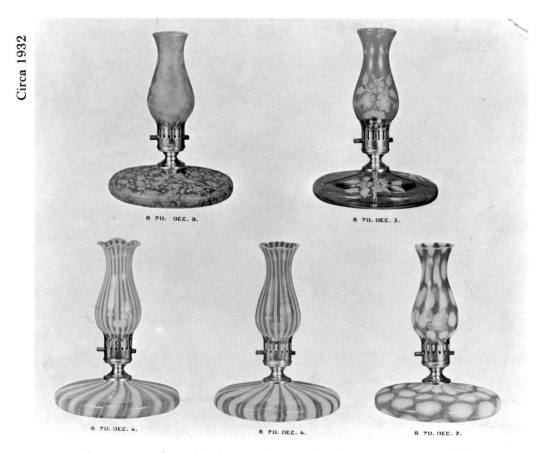

Assortment of boudoir lamps, decorated and opalescent, circa 1932.

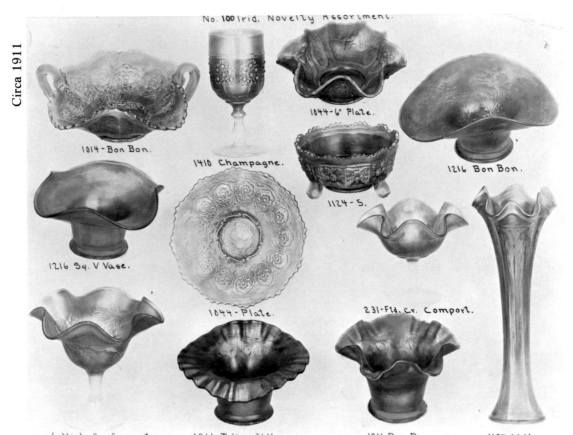

Assortment of iridescent novelties, including *Persian Medallion* (#1014, 1044), *Orange Tree* (#1410), *Sailboats* (#1044), *Blackberry Spray* (#1216), *Carnival Holly* (#1216, top right), *Rib & Holly Sprig* (#231), *Butterfly & Berry* (#1124) and *Peacock & Urn* (bottom left).

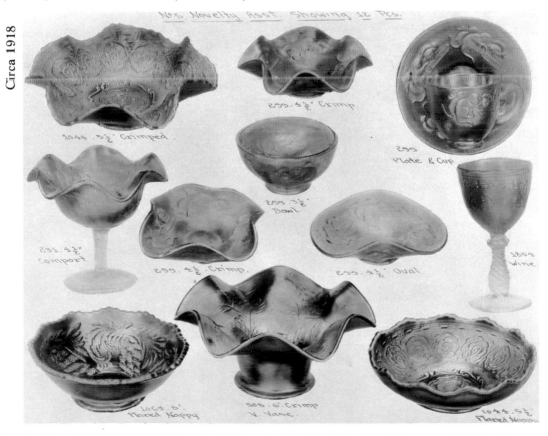

Assortment of carnival glass novelties, including the popular *Kittens* miniatures (#299), *Persian Medallion* (#1044), *Rib & Holly Sprig* (#231), *Pine Cone* (#1064), *Carnival Holly* (#508).

Early advertisement for Fenton's art glass line of *Hanging Heart* and *Hanging Vine,* circa 1926.

The Fenton Art Glass Company
Miscellaneous Catalog Reprints

1565--1538 Turtle Aquarium
SOMETHING NEW IN THE NOVELTY LINE?
HERE IT IS
Large Green Glass Turtle with full half gallon aquarium in clear crystal "Bubble" glass.
EVERYBODY IS BUYING IT
Price complete, bowl and base $15.00 per Dozen.   Packs 1½ Dozen to $1.25 barrel.
THE FENTON ART GLASS COMPANY
Williamstown, W. Va.

The Fenton Art Glass Co. - Williamstown, W. Va.

No. 1565—TURTLE
Covered Bon Bon or Flower Bowl.   Made in plain
green only.   Size 9 inches.

No. 1564—TURTLE FLOWER BLOCK
8 holes.   Size 4 inches.   Made in various colors.

**Illustrated above are ads dating about 1929 illus-
trating Fenton's figural Turtles, including the rare
aquarium (above right).**

No. 208. Cut Water Set. Packs 1 dozen sets to barrel.

No. 209. Cut Water Set. Packs 1 dozen sets to barrel.

No. 211. Cut Water Set. Packs 1 dozen sets to barrel.

No. 210. Cut Water Set. Packs 1 dozen sets to barrel.

▲ Assortment of crystal water sets in a variety of cut designs.

A wide variety of Fenton's #400 series (400-412) made in crystal with very limited production in chocolate glass. ▼

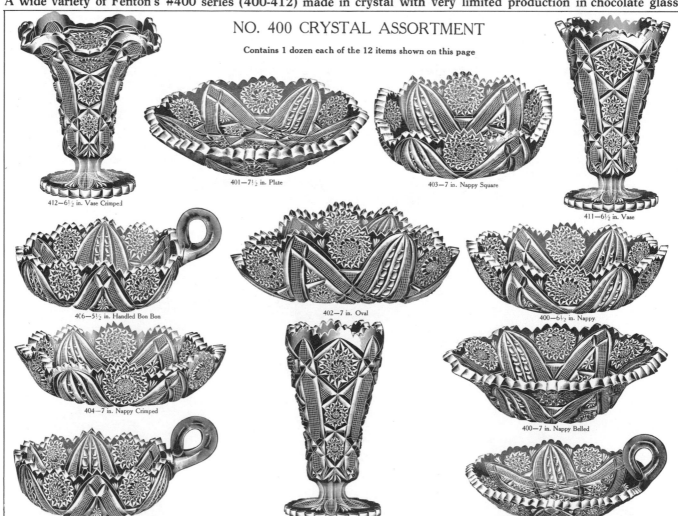

NO. 400 CRYSTAL ASSORTMENT

Contains 1 dozen each of the 12 items shown on this page

412—6½ in. Vase Crimped

401—7½ in. Plate

403—7 in. Nappy Square

411—6½ in. Vase

406—5½ in. Handled Bon Bon

402—7 in. Oval

400—6½ in. Nappy

404—7 in. Nappy Crimped

400—7 in. Nappy Belled

407—6 in. Handled Bon Bon Tripod

OUR "ARISTOCRAT" LINE OF BUD VASES

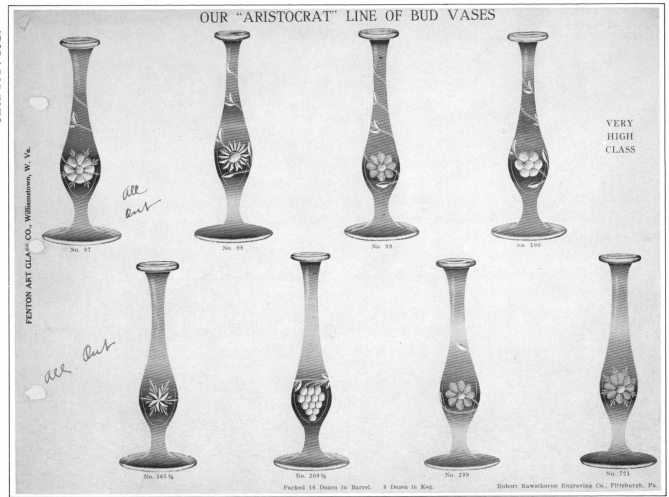

FENTON ART GLASS CO., Williamstown, W. Va.

VERY
HIGH
CLASS

No. 97

No. 98

No. 99

No. 100

No. 165½

No. 209½

No. 299

No. 721

Packed 16 Dozen In Barrel.   8 Dozen in Keg.   Robert Rawsthorne Engraving Co., Pittsburgh, Pa.

Assortment of cutting designs in Fenton's "Aristocrat" bud vases in crystal.

FENTON ART GLASS CO., WILLIAMSTOWN, W. VA.

No. 125 Cut Water Set

Grape Design

Robert Rawsthorne Eng. Co., Pittsburgh, Pa.

Fenton's #125 Grape designed cut water set.

9 IN. REGULAR
4 DOZ. IN BBL. BBLS. 50C.
PER DOZ. 80C.

10 IN SCALLOPED.
4 DOZ. IN BBL. BBLS. 50C.
PER DOZ. 80C.

11 IN. FLAT PLATE.
4 DOZ. IN BBL. BBLS. 50C.
PER DOZ. 80C.

The *Northern Star* bowl and plate, incorrectly attributed to Northwood in my book on opalescent glass. This was made in crystal, carnival and opalescent colors.

Fenton's #1134 *Cherry & Scale* pattern in custard glass—called *Fentonia Fruit* in carnival glass.

Assortment of green and crystal enamel-decorated water sets.

Assortment of water sets in decorated glass, including #821 "Cannonball" pitcher.

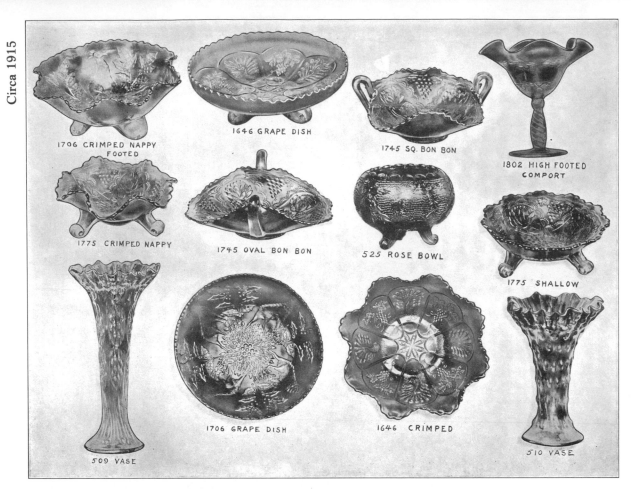

1706 CRIMPED NAPPY FOOTED

1646 GRAPE DISH

1745 SQ. BON BON

1802 HIGH FOOTED COMPORT

1775 CRIMPED NAPPY

1745 OVAL BON BON

525 ROSE BOWL

1775 SHALLOW

509 VASE

1706 GRAPE DISH

1646 CRIMPED

510 VASE

Wide variety of carnival novelties, including #1706 *Stag & Holly*, #1646 *Peacock & Grape*, #1745 *Lotus & Grape*, #1802 *Sailboats*, #1775 footed *Lotus & Grape*, #525 *Garlands*, #509 *Knotted Beads* vase, and #510 *Rustic* vase.

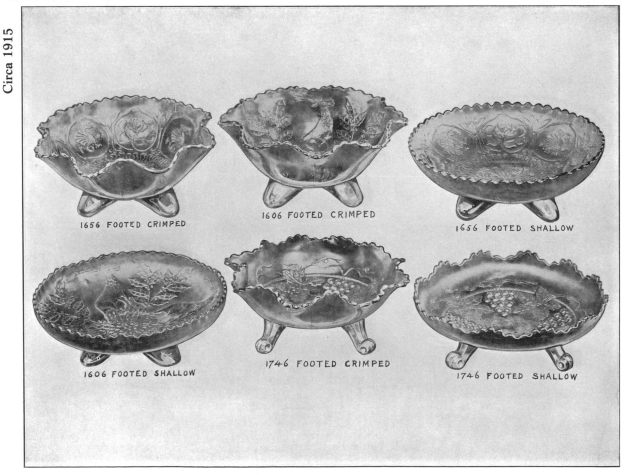

1656 FOOTED CRIMPED

1606 FOOTED CRIMPED

1656 FOOTED SHALLOW

1606 FOOTED SHALLOW

1746 FOOTED CRIMPED

1746 FOOTED SHALLOW

Assortment of carnival novelties, including #1656 *Dragon & Lotus*, #1606 *Stag and Holly* and #1746 footed *Grape & Cable*.

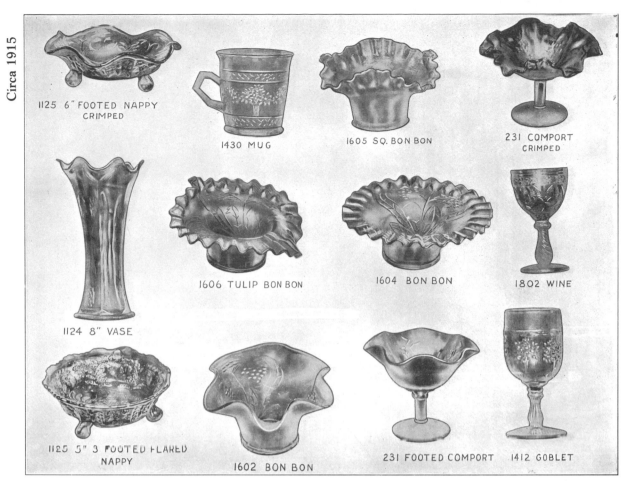

1125 6" FOOTED NAPPY CRIMPED

1430 MUG

1605 SQ. BON BON

231 COMPORT CRIMPED

1124 8" VASE

1606 TULIP BON BON

1604 BON BON

1802 WINE

1125 5" 3 FOOTED FLARED NAPPY

1602 BON BON

231 FOOTED COMPORT

1412 GOBLET

Assortment of carnival novelties, including #1124-1125 *Butterfly & Berry* vase and nappy, #1430 *Orange Tree*, #1602-1606 *Flowering Dill* bon-bons, #1802 *Sailboats*, #1125 *Panther*, and #1412 *Orange Tree*, #231 *Rib & Holly Sprig* compote.

350

351

352

Assortment of Fenton opalescent mold-blown pitchers and pressed tumblers; (l. to r.) *Fenton Drapery, Buttons & Braids* and *Coinspot.*

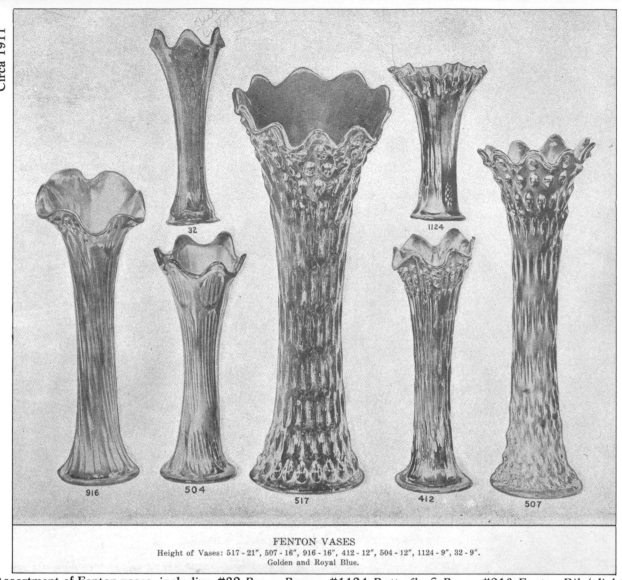

FENTON VASES
Height of Vases: 517 - 21″, 507 - 16″, 916 - 16″, 412 - 12″, 504 - 12″, 1124 - 9″, 32 - 9″.
Golden and Royal Blue.

Assortment of Fenton vases, including #32 *Boggy Bayou*, #1124 *Butterfly & Berry*, #916 *Fenton Rib* (slightly twisted), #504 *Diamond & Rib*, #507 & 517 *Rustic*, and #412 *April Showers*.

Assortment of Fenton carnival novelties, including #1695 *Two Fruits*, #1802 *Sailboats*, #47 *Daisy Cut Bell*, #1401 & #1416 *Orange Tree*, #1192 *Fenton Basket* with *Blackberry* interior, #922 *Vintage* and #1124 *Butterfly & Berry*.

Assortment of *Leaf Tiers* pattern in carnival glass. The mold for the bowl was later revived for production in red slag, frosted crystal, milk glass, etc. (See page 112 & 114).

Carnival glass water sets in #1563 *Lattice & Grape*, #1561 *Apple Tree* and #1562 *Blueberry*.

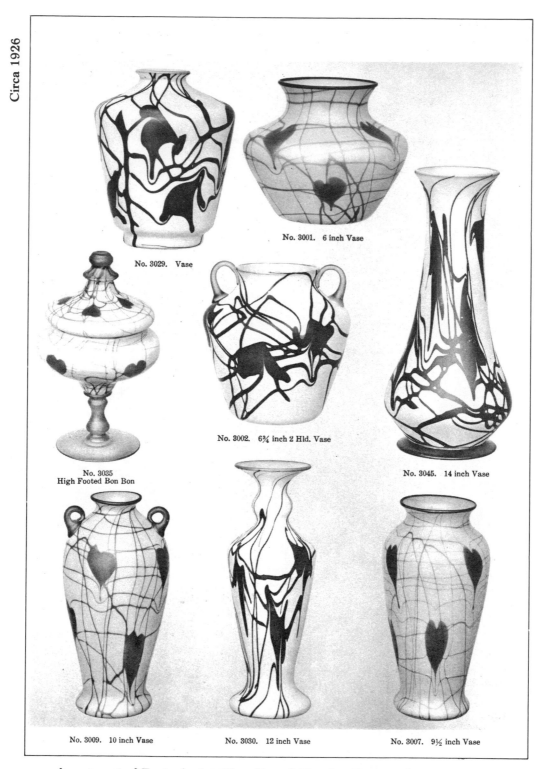

No. 3029. Vase

No. 3001. 6 inch Vase

No. 3035
High Footed Bon Bon

No. 3002. 6¾ inch 2 Hld. Vase

No. 3045. 14 inch Vase

No. 3009. 10 inch Vase

No. 3030. 12 inch Vase

No. 3007. 9½ inch Vase

Assortment of Fenton's Art Glass line of *Hanging Heart* and *Hanging Vine*.

No. 3016
9 inch Footed Bowl

No. 3012.   4 inch Vase

No. 3037.   Cov. Bon Bon

No. 3005.   5½ inch Vase

No. 3039.   Footed Vase

No. 3014.   4 inch Vase

No. 3013.   6 inch Vase

No. 3000.   11 inch Vase

No. 3006.   10 inch Vase

ABOVE ITEMS IN 3 FINISHES, KARNAK RED, MOSAIC INLAID, ORIENTAL IVORY,
ALL OFF HAND.   HIGH CLASS GLASSWARE.

More items in Fenton's Art Glass lines of hand-made quality items.

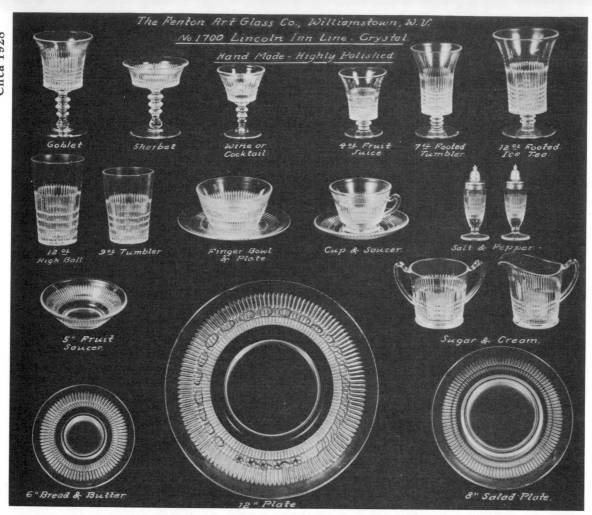

The Fenton Art Glass Co., Williamstown, W.V.
No 1700 Lincoln Inn Line - Crystal.
Hand Made - Highly Polished

Goblet   Sherbet   Wine or Cocktail   4 oz Fruit Juice   7 oz Footed Tumbler   12 oz Footed Ice Tea.

12 oz High Ball   9 oz Tumbler   Finger Bowl & Plate   Cup & Saucer.   Salt & Pepper.

5" Fruit Saucer.   Sugar & Cream.

6" Bread & Butter.   12" Plate   8" Salad Plate.

FENTON ART GLASS COMPANY
WILLIAMSTOWN, W. VA.
No. 1700 Line in Rose, Green, and Aquamarine.

1700 Goblet   1700 Sherbet   1700S Oval   1700S Nut   1700S Mint

1700 Cream   1700 Sugar   1700 Cup and Saucer   1700 Cereal

1700 Hdl. Olive   1700-S Hdl. Bon Bon Square   1700-S Hdl. Bon Bon Oval   1700-C 6" Crimp

1700 12" Plate   1700 8" Plate   1700-G Comport Plate   1700-G Shallow Comport

Assortment of Fenton's #1700 *Lincoln Inn* line made in crystal and color.

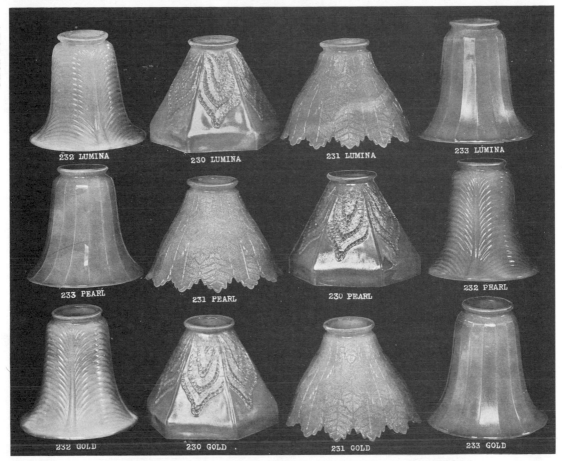

Assortment of iridescent glass shades made by Fenton about 1914.

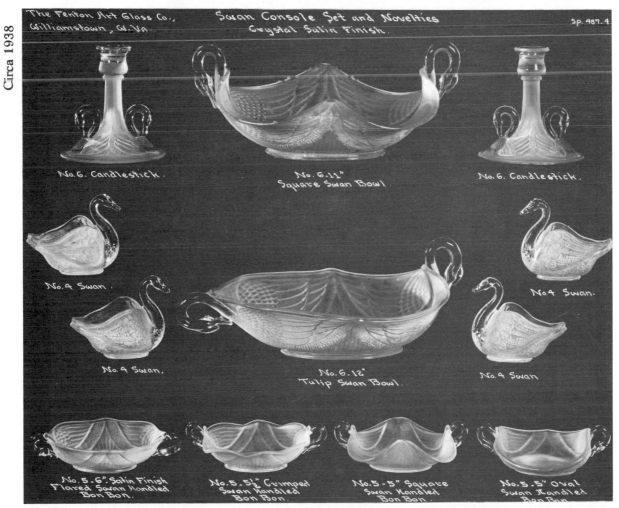

Even though the ad dates after 1932, it is reprinted here to show you substantial proof that Fenton also made the *Little Swan* novelties, reportedly from the original Northwood molds. Shown here in frosted crystal.

109

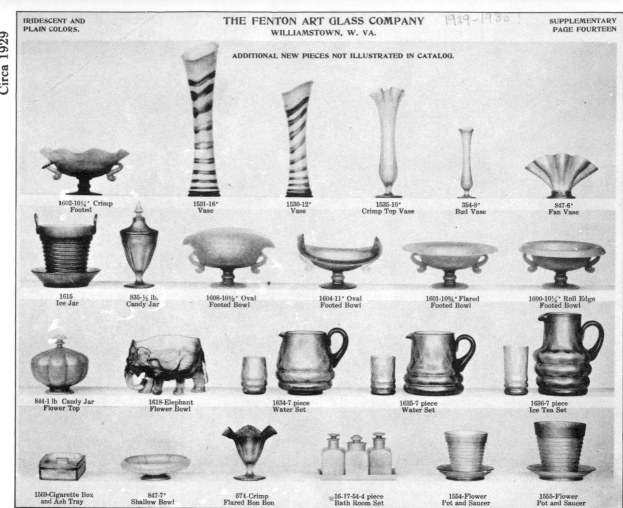

THE FENTON ART GLASS COMPANY
WILLIAMSTOWN, W. VA.

1929-1930

ADDITIONAL NEW PIECES NOT ILLUSTRATED IN CATALOG.

1602-10¼" Crimp Footed

1531-16" Vase

1530-12" Vase

1535-10" Crimp Top Vase

354-8" Bud Vase

847-6" Fan Vase

1615 Ice Jar

835-½ lb. Candy Jar

1608-10½" Oval Footed Bowl

1604-11" Oval Footed Bowl

1601-10¾" Flared Footed Bowl

1600-10⅛" Roll Edge Footed Bowl

844-1 lb Candy Jar Flower Top

1618-Elephant Flower Bowl

1634-7 piece Water Set

1635-7 piece Water Set

1636-7 piece Ice Tea Set

1569-Cigarette Box and Ash Tray

847-7" Shallow Bowl

574-Crimp Flared Bon Bon

16-17-54-4 piece Bath Room Set

1554-Flower Pot and Saucer

1555-Flower Pot and Saucer

▲ Wide assortment of Fenton wares made in iridescent (stretch) and plain colors—note the unique elephant flower bowl. Wide assortment of Fenton colored ware with cut or engraved designs.▼

THE FENTON ART GLASS COMPANY
WILLIAMSTOWN, W. VA.
Cut and Engraved Novelties, in Rose, Green, and Aquamarine.

Introduced 1929 - FM

1621-1703 Crimp Bon Bon

1621-1703-Square Bon Bon

1621-1703 Plate Bon Bon

1640-1702 9 oz. Bridge Goblet

1641-1702 11 oz. Ice Tea

1642-1702 Goblet

1621-1703 Bon Bon

1614-1702 Ice Pack

1616-1702 Ice Pack

1532A-1702 Fan Vase

1533 A 1702 Fan Vase

1533 A 1702 Candy Jar

1502-1702 8" Flip Vase

318-1702 Candle Stick

1504-A 9½" Fld. Cup Bowl

318-1702 Candle Stick

1504-A 9" Flared

16

1634-1702 Water Set

1635-1702 Water Set

1636-1702 Ice Tea Set

THE FENTON ART GLASS COMPANY, WILLIAMSTOWN, W. VA.
No. 1502 DIAMOND OPTIC LINE, MADE ONLY IN PLAIN ROSE, PLAIN GREEN AND ORCHID COLORS.

No. 1502. 7 inch Roll Edge Vase.
No. 1502. 8 inch Crimp Top Vase.
No. 1502. 8½ inch Fan Vase.
No. 1502. 6 inch Dolphin 2 Hdl. Fan Vase.
No. 1502. 5½ inch Dolphin 2 Hdl. Fan Vase.
No. 1502. 6 inch Flared Vase.
No. 1502. 8½ inch Flared Vase.

No. 1502. 7½ inch Comport Bon Bon.
No. 1502. 7½ inch Oval Bon Bon.
No. 1502. 6 inch Flared Bon Bon.
No. 1502. 7½ inch Crimp Top Bon Bon.
No. 1502. 3 Piece Dresser Set.

No. 53. 4 Piece Dresser Set.
No. 1502. 12 inch 3 Piece Console Set Special Roll Edge Bowl.

No. 1502. 13 inch Flared Bowl.
No. 1502. 10 inch Cupped No. 1502. 12 inch Cupped Bowl.
No. 1502. 10 inch Hdl. Sandwich Tray

No. 1502 8 inch Octagon Salad Plate.
No. 1502 Footed Sherbet.
No. 1502 Goblet
No. 1502 Cup and Saucer
No. 1502. Sugar and Cream Set.
No. 1502. Mayonnaise and Ladle.
No. 1502. Cheese and Cracker.

▲ Wide assortment of *Diamond Optic* line, and also (below) *Spiral Optic* line. The catalogue states they were made
▼ only in plain colors, but examples of stretch glass items have been found.

THE FENTON ART GLASS COMPANY
WILLIAMSTOWN, W. VA.
1502 DIAMOND AND 1503 SPIRAL OPTIC LINE.
Plain Colors — Rose — Green — Orchid — Royal Blue — Ruby

SUPPLEMENTARY
PAGE THIRTEEN

1502A-8" Flared Cup Bowl
1502A-7" Cupped Bowl
1502A-9" Crimp Bowl
1503A-8½" Roll Edge Bowl
1503A-7" Cupped Bowl

1502A-8½" Roll Edge Bowl
1502 8½" Flared Cup Bowl
1502-14" Special Roll Edge Bowl
1503 Candlestick
1503-10" Flared Bowl
1503 Candlestick

1502-10" Special Roll Edge Bowl
1502A-10" Flared Bowl
1502-8" Deep Cup Bowl
1623 Candlestick
1503A-10" Flared Bowl
1623 Candlestick
1503A-9" Shallow Cup Bowl

1502 Cup and Saucer

1502-2 pc. Guest Set
1502-11 oz. Bridge Goblet
1502-9" Bridge Goblet
1502-Finger Bowl and Plate
1502-6" Octagon Plate
1503-8" Spiral Optic Plate
1503-Spiral Optic Sherbet
1503-9 oz. Goblet

111

Circa 1934

Circa 1933

Wide assortment of items in Fenton satin crystal and milk glass.

No.14-12 Pce. Flint Opalescent Assortment.

1790.10"
Flared Bowl.

1790.7"
Cupped Bowl.

950.11"
Oval Bowl.

920.11"
Flared Bowl.

901.8"
Crimped Vase

901.
Fan Vase.

901.5¼"
Square Vase.

901.6½"
Flared Vase.

901.9½"
Crimped Vase.

920-9"
Cupped Bowl

1790.12"
Plate

920.10".
Crimped Bowl.

Assortment of white opalescent Fenton glass, including Grape & Cable bowl and Leaf Tiers 12" plate which I incorrectly attributed to Northwood in my opalescent book.

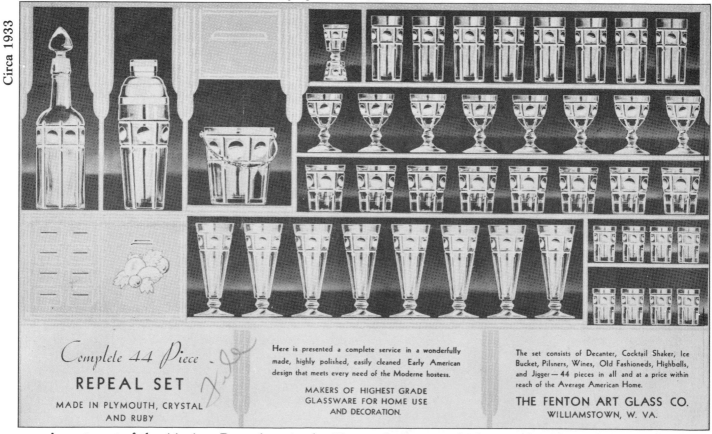

Complete 44 Piece

REPEAL SET

MADE IN PLYMOUTH, CRYSTAL AND RUBY

Here is presented a complete service in a wonderfully made, highly polished, easily cleaned Early American design that meets every need of the Moderne hostess.

MAKERS OF HIGHEST GRADE GLASSWARE FOR HOME USE AND DECORATION.

The set consists of Decanter, Cocktail Shaker, Ice Bucket, Pilsners, Wines, Old Fashioneds, Highballs, and Jigger — 44 pieces in all and at a price within reach of the Average American Home.

THE FENTON ART GLASS CO.
WILLIAMSTOWN, W. VA.

Assortment of the 44-piece Repeal set in the *Plymouth* pattern which was advertised after the repeal of prohibition.

Butler Brothers Ads

Featuring Fenton Glass

CONFIRMATIVE FENTON: Items which can be confirmed as Fenton Glass by their appearance in existing catalogues.

PROBABLE FENTON: Items which do not appear in existing early catalogues, but can be attributed to Fenton by their inclusion in Butler Brothers groupings.

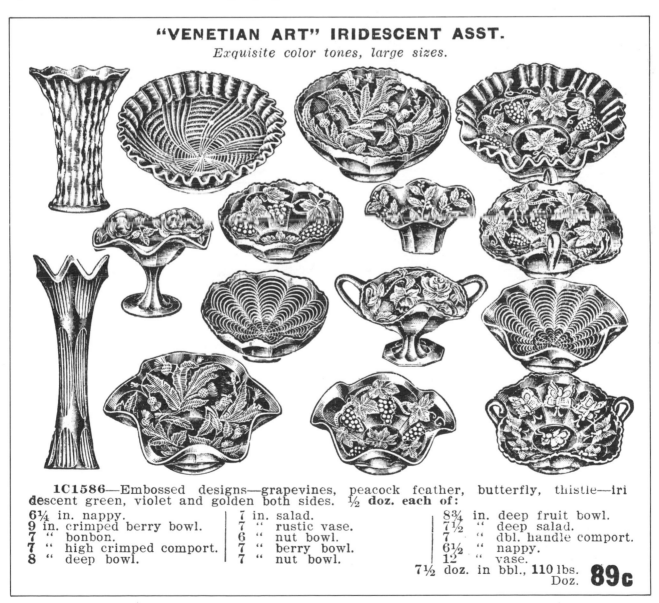

"VENETIAN ART" IRIDESCENT ASST.

Exquisite color tones, large sizes.

1C1586—Embossed designs—grapevines, peacock feather, butterfly, thistle—iridescent green, violet and golden both sides. ½ doz. each of:

6¼ in. nappy.	7 in. salad.	8¾ in. deep fruit bowl.
9 in. crimped berry bowl.	7 " rustic vase.	7½ " deep salad.
7 " bonbon.	6 " nut bowl.	7 " dbl. handle comport.
7 " high crimped comport.	7 " berry bowl.	6½ " nappy.
8 " deep bowl.	7 " nut bowl.	12 " vase.

7½ doz. in bbl., 110 lbs.
Doz. **89c**

GROUP A (Circa 1910) Several patterns in the above Butler Brothers catalogue can be properly attributed to Fenton because of this grouping. CONFIRMATIVE FENTON: *Vintage, Diamond & Rib, Rustic Vase, Peacock Tail*, PROBABLE FENTON: *Carnival Thistle, Butterflies, Ribbon Tie, Wreath of Roses* compotes and bon-bons.

VENETIAN ART COMPORT ASST—Iridescent.

These exceptional sellers in still more attractive designs and color effects.

1C1854—6 high foot styles, diam. 5¾ to 7 in., fruit, wild rose, iris, blackberry and feather embossed, violet, royal blue, green and golden bodies, allover sunset metallic iridescent. ⅔ doz. each shape, 4 doz. in bbl., lbs. **Doz. 87c**

GROUP B (1910) CONFIRMATIVE FENTON: *Peacock Tail, Vintage.* PROBABLE FENTON: *Iris* compote (also made in goblet).

1C2418— Fine quality glass bodies, rich embossed floral, leaf, fruit and conventional designs, golden and royal blue iridescent finished in fired colors. ⅛ doz. each of the following:

Asstd. 4 doz. in bbl., 78 lbs. **Doz $2.10** (Total $8.40)

GROUP C (Circa 1920) CONFIRMATIVE FENTON: *Horse Medallion, Orange Tree, Two Fruits, Grape & Cable, Peacock & Urn, Fenton Rib* vase, *April Showers, Butterfly & Berry, Carnival Holly.* PROBABLE FENTON: *Plaid* bowl.

ZF5565. Full sizes, golden iridescent ware; heavy embossed flower and fruit designs. Assortment comprises—

One dozen 7-inch Vases.
One dozen 5-inch Footed Nut Dishes.
One dozen 5¼-inch Wine Glasses.
One dozen 5-inch Crimped Comports.
One dozen 5¾-inch Footed Bonbons.
One dozen 4½-inch Clarets.
One dozen 6¼-inch Fancy Olives.
One dozen 3½-inch Mugs.
One dozen 4½-inch Footed Jellies.
One dozen 6-inch Crimped Preserve Dishes.
One dozen 6-inch Square Dishes.
One dozen 6½-inch Flared Bonbons.
  Total, 12 dozen to a barrel.....................DOZ., .42
Shipped from West Virginia.

GROUP D (Circa 1920) CONFIRMATIVE FENTON: *Butterfly & Berry* bowl, *Orange Tree* claret, *Orange Tree* mug, *Sailboats* wine, *Flowering Dill* novelties. PROBABLE FENTON: *Wide Panel* vase.

Generally sold for twice what we ask.

2411—Full size, heavy embossing, asst. comprises:
1 doz. 8 in. vases.
1 " 4¾ in. jellies.
1 " 7 in. deep bowls.
1 " crimped bonbons, 7 in.
1 doz. 3½ in. hdld mugs.
1 " 6½ in. berry dishes.
1 " 7½ in. cake plates.
1 " 6 in. crimped table dishes.
1 doz. 7½ oz. table tumblers.
1 " 5½ in. preserve dishes.
1 " 8 in. vases, royal tinted.
1 " 6 in. nut bowls.
(Total for asst. $6.84) 12 doz. in bbl., about 128 lbs. **Doz. 57c**

GROUP E (Circa 1920) CONFIRMATIVE FENTON: *Peacock & Dahlia, Orange Tree, Banded Blackberry, Sailboats, Lattice & Grape* tumbler, *Butterfly & Berry* vase? PROBABLE FENTON: *Lion* (Stalking Lion).

116

Oval 2-handled Bonbons, 7¼-inch.
Footed Crimped Bowl, 7½-inch.
Footed Shallow Bowl, 7½-inch.
Crimped and Flared Top Vase, 6¾-inch.
Shallow Flat Nappie, 6¼-inch.
Crimped Fruit Dish, 8¾-inch.
    Total, 12 dozen to a barrel....................................DOZ., .72
    Shipped from Williamstown, W. Va.

Footed Scalloped Nappie, 6-inch.
Crimped Comport, 5½x6¼-inch.
Footed Rose Bowl, 5-inch.
Square 2-handled Nut Bowl, 5¼-inch.
Footed Crimped Berry Dish, 7½-inch.
Tall Flared Top Vase, 10-inch.

GROUP F (Circa 1920) CON-FIRMATIVE FENTON: *Garlands* rose bowl, *Knotted Beads* vase, *Stag & Holly* footed bowl, *Sailboats, Two Flowers* 3-footed bowl. **PROBABLE FENTON:** *Lotus & Grape* footed bowl, 2-hdl bon-bon, *Thistle & Lotus* bowl.

"AURORA" GLASSWARE ASSORTMENT—Iridescent
Surpassing value. Includes pieces never before found in an assortment at this price.

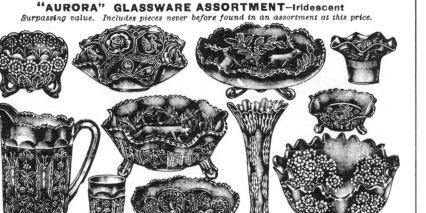

C2413 — Practical items, floral, Persian, fruit cluster and peacock embossing, rich golden iridescent finish. Comprises:

4 only 11½ in. massive footed orange bowls.	6 only 8 in. sauce or fruit bowls.
9 " 9 in. footed berry bowls.	6 " 8 " vases.
12 " 4¼ in. nappies to match.	6 " 5 " rose bowls.
2 " ½ gal. jugs.	6 " 6 " footed nut bowls.
12 " 7 oz. tumblers to match.	6 " 10 in. crimped vases.
4 " 10 in. flared footed bowls.	12 " 3½ in. handled mugs.
4 " 10 " crimp " "	12 " 5½ in. crimped bonbons.
6 " 9 in. crimp salad dishes.	
(Total for asst. $8.50) 100 pc. in bbl., 147 lbs.	Each, **8½c**

GROUP G (Circa 1920) CON-FIRMATIVE FENTON: *Fenton Flowers, Stag & Holly, Blackberry Banded, Butterfly & Berry* assortment, *Orange Tree* footed orange bowl, *Dragon & Lotus, Peacock & Grape.*

NEW VENETIAN ART ASS'T — Iridescent
Large artistic designs, glazed, iridescent finishings.

GROUP H (1910) CONFIRMATIVE FENTON: *Diamond & Rib* vase, *Vintage* bowl & bon-bons, *Blackberry Bramble, Peacock Tail* compotes. **PROBABLE FENTON:** *Ragged Robin, Autumn Acorn, Butterflies.*

MAMMOTH GOLDEN ASSORTMENT

Extra sizes in fancy shaped glassware, heavily embossed, floral and conventional designs, iridescent finish.

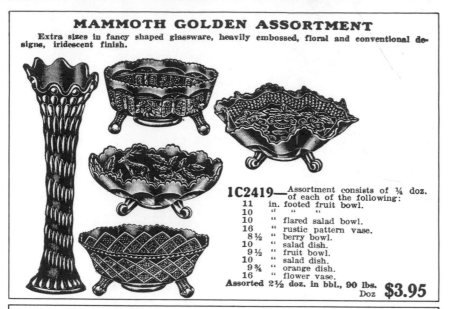

1C2419—Assortment consists of ¼ doz. of each of the following:

11	in.	footed fruit bowl.
10	"	" "
10	"	flared salad bowl.
16	"	rustic pattern vase.
8½	"	berry bowl.
10	"	salad dish.
9½	"	fruit bowl.
10	"	salad dish.
9¾	"	orange dish.
16	"	flower vase.

Assorted 2½ doz. in bbl., 90 lbs.

Doz **$3.95**

"ENORMOUS" IRIDESCENT GLASSWARE BARGAIN.

A TREMENDOUS BARGAIN. SUITABLE FOR ANY BARGAIN COUNTER.

ZF5546. Three styles. 8¼-inch footed bowl, with scalloped edge; 8¼-inch footed bowl, with crimped and scalloped edge; footed rose bowl, 5½x4¼ inches, with scalloped edge. Fancy embossed fruit or flower designs, gilded and royal blue iridescent, metallic lustre, massive, heavy glass. Total, 6 doz. asstd. to bbl...........................DOZ., .81
Shipped from West Virginia.

Floral and Grape Embossed Asst. – 2 styles, golden iridescent, 11 in. plain top tankard and 9 in. crimped top squat blown jugs, cap. ½ gal., stuck handles, SIX 9 oz. tumblers to match. 3 sets each,

C1868 – Asstd. 6 sets in bbl., 53 lbs.   Set, **68c**
(Total $4.08)

Grapevine Embossed—Jug, ht. 11½ in., ½ gal., SIX 9 oz. tumblers, relief grape clusters and lattice embossing, golden iridescent finish.

C1871—6 sets in bbl., 70 lbs.
(Total $4.50)   Set, **75c**

C2248—2 sets in carton
(Total $1.54)   Set, **77c**

GROUP I (1925) These are all confirmed Fenton patterns: *Rustic* vase, and bowls in *Butterfly and Berry, Two Flowers, Stag & Holly,* and *Fentonia Fruit.*

GROUP J (Circa 1920) Shown here are two variations of Fenton's *Grape and Cable* footed bowl, and the *Fenton Flowers* nut bowl. Note the ad states "shipped from West Virginia".

GROUP K (Circa 1915) Here are illustrated three Fenton water sets originally sold for an unbelievable price per set (wholesale). *Floral and Grape* and *Lattice & Grape* are confirmed Fenton patterns— *Lattice & Daisy* can thus be somewhat confirmed as well.

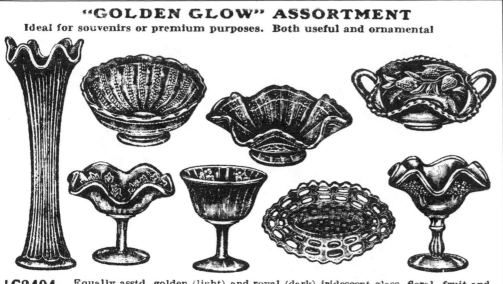

"GOLDEN GLOW" ASSORTMENT
Ideal for souvenirs or premium purposes. Both useful and ornamental

1C2404—Equally asstd. golden (light) and royal (dark) iridescent glass, floral, fruit and fancy paneled designs. 1 doz. each of the following pieces:

7	in.	tulip bonbon dishes.	7	in. 3 footed crimped nappies.
5¾	"	footed comports.	7¾	" crimped footed nappies.
6	"	high footed crimped comports.	8	" flared fancy plates.
7½	"	crimped violet vases.	10	" fancy flower vases.
6½	"	flared footed bowls.	7¾	" tulip bonbons.
6	"	square double handled bonbons.	5¾	" high footed crimped comports.

Assorted 12 doz. in bbl., 122 lbs. Doz **95c**
(Total $11.40)

IRIDESCENT DINING SET ASSORTMENT

2 Water Sets — 2 Table Sets
2 Salad or Berry Sets.

1C1766—"Golden Glow," golden iridescent finish, embossed butterfly and grape design. Big full sized extra heavy sets of extreme richness. Asst. comprises 6 sets as follows, all pieces to match:

TWO 7 PC. WATER SETS—	TWO 7 PC. BERRY SETS—	TWO 4 PC. TABLE SETS
Two ½ gal. jugs.	Two 8½ in. bowls.	2 creamers. | 2 butters.
Twelve 8 oz. tumblers.	Twelve 5 in. nappies.	2 sugars. | 2 spoon holders.

Asstd. 6 sets in bbl., 70 lbs. SET **$1.20**
(Total $7.20)

IRIDESCENT BERRY BOWL ASSORTMENT

1C1920—4 styles, average 9½ in. diam., golden iridescent, imitation cu floral and leaf and embossed figure and floral designs, crimped and scalloped edges. Asstd. 2 doz. in case, 40 lbs......Doz **$2.1**

"Marvelous" Rose-Pink

1C-2419—12 different pieces, fine quality, full finished rose-pink glass, rich embossed floral, leaf and fruit designs.

¼ doz. each of the following:

Salad Dish—8¾ in., crimped edge.
Candy Dish—6 in., handled.
Fruit Bowl—8½ in., flared.
Flower Vase—11½ in., rustic
Bonbon Dish—9 in., handled.
Salad Dish—8¼ in., footed.

Fruit Bowl—9 in., crimped edge.
Bonbon Dish—8 in., 3 feet.
Bowl—6½ in., deep, 3 feet.
Fruit Bowl—8 in., 3 feet.
Vase—12 in., tall, ribbed.
Fruit Bowl—8½ in., deep, footed.

Asstd. 3 doz. in barrel, 75 lbs.................**Doz $1.95**
(Total $5.85)

GROUP O (1930) Quite suddenly, iridescent carnival glass disappeared from the Butler Brothers catalogues in 1930. However, old molds were used in a new line of rose pink colored glass. In this group we find: *April Showers* vase, *Horse Medallions, Stippled Rays, Fenton's Holly, Cherry Circles, Orange Tree, Butterfly & Berry,* and *Two Fruits.*

Novelty Glassware—IN COLORS

21 Different Pieces—Artistic shapes and fancy designs in popular transparent glass.

1 doz. each of the following:

Flower Vase—10 in.
Mug—3½ in. high (9 oz.), handled
Nappy—6¾ in., footed
Card Receptacle—6¼ in., handled
Table Dish—6¼ in., footed
Bud Vase—8½ in., footed

Violet Vase—6½ in., footed
Comport—5 in., footed
Nappy—6 in., 3 feet
Comport—4 in. high, footed, flared
Bonbon Dish—6¾ in., turned up edge
Nappy — 6½ in., handled, rolled-up edge

Asstd. 12 doz. in barrel, 120 lbs.

1C1321—EMERALD GREEN..............⎫ **Doz**
1C1322—ROSE PINK..................⎬ **92c**
(Total $11.04)　　　　　　　　　　　⎭

GROUP P (1930) Also, in this late catalogue, we find early carnival patterns offered in rose pink and emerald green. This group includes: *Fenton Rib* vase, *Blackberry Spray, Orange Tree, Rib & Holly Sprig, Blackberry Banded.*

Miscellaneous Fenton

Needless to say, as thorough as this book appears to be, there are some rare items which we were unable to locate for photographing. Also, much early Fenton never appeared in catalogues, and inventory listings do little to describe their production. We plan on including a "wrap-up" section of early rarities in the proposed sequel. Until then, here are a few items which we missed in the color portion of this book.

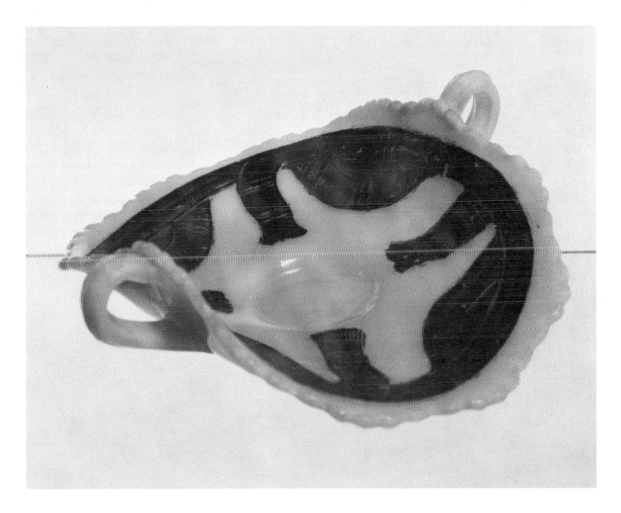

Custard Glass 2-handled Bon-Bon in "Prayer Rug" pattern, which I incorrectly attributed to Imperial in my Book 4. It is rare in marigold iridescense over custard glass, and would be very rare in dark carnival.

Figure A—Previously unlisted *Rib and Holly Sprig* compote in blue.

Figure B—Scarce *Orange Tree* jelly compote in marigold—also made in dark carnival and non-iridescent colors.

Figure C—Scarce vaseline opalescent *Lattice & Daisy* small berry, which is rare in carnival colors.

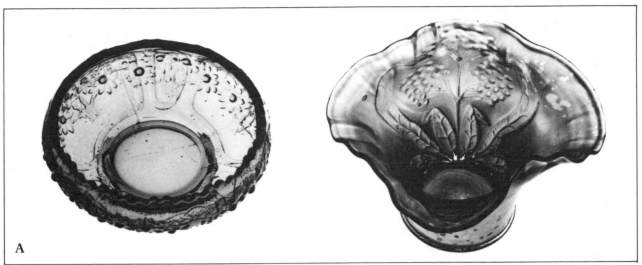

A

Figure A—Unusual amber (non-iridescent) *Sailboats* nappy with *Orange Tree* exterior, and marigold *Flowering Dill* bon-bon.

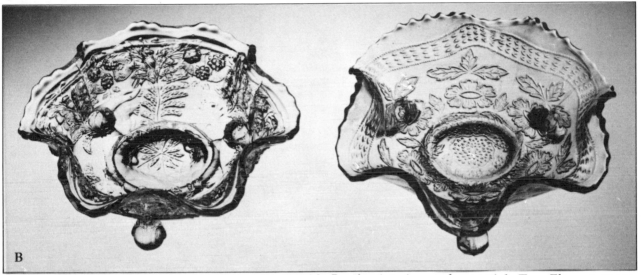

B

Figure B—Unusual clear *Butterfly & Berry* nappy with *Panther* interior, and rose pink *Two Flowers* nappy.

C

Figure C—Rare chocolate glass #410 *Fenton Sunburst* vase (top polished); also scarce chocolate puff jar and hatpin holder in *Orange Tree*.

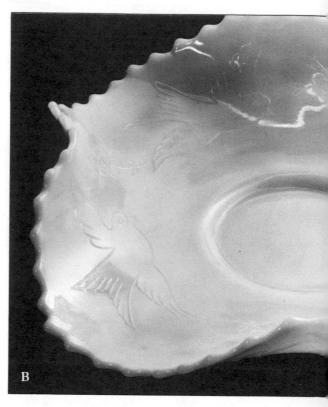

Figure A—Popular Fenton back (reverse) pattern known as *Bearded Berry,* shown on back of several Fenton patterns and a primary source of attribution.

Figure B—Close-up photograph of the Fenton *Bluebirds* bowl showing the pattern detail which was lost in the color illustration shown in my custard glass book—this pattern can also be found goofus decorated.

Figure C — Custard Glass *Blackberry Spray* bon-bon with goofus decoration.

Miscellaneous Fenton

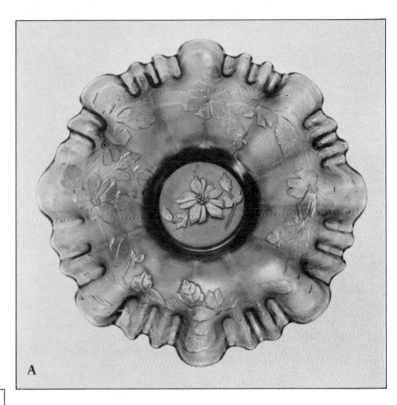

Figure A—*Ragged Robin* bowl, attributed to Fenton by Butler Brothers 1910 Catalogue on page 117.

Figure B—Marigold *Knotted Beads* vase, shown in 1915 Fenton catalogue on page 102.

Figure—Shown above is a most unusual large crimped bowl in *Wreath of Roses* (back pattern) with a *Vintage* interior, formed from the top of a punch bowl.

The cutting department, circa 1907—note the Coinspot and Swirl pitchers and the Boggy Bayou vases in opalescent glass on the table at right.

Decorating room, circa 1907—note the incandescent bulbs hanging overhead.

types of colors, the two most famous being chocolate (now called "caramel slag") and golden agate. It was in the course of these wanderings that Rosenthal spent some time at the Northwood plant in Indiana, Pennsylvania, and came to know young Frank Fenton. It was there also that a Rosenthal cousin, Charles Brand, married a Fenton sister, Gertrude, thus linking the two families not only professionally, but also genealogically.

In 1898, Rosenthal came to Marietta to work in the Royal Glass Company, located in the city's east end. He left Royal in 1900, after serving a number of months as superintendent, and moved to Greentown, Indiana, home of the Indiana Tumbler and Goblet Company. Indiana Tumbler burned down in 1903, ostensibly when sparks from a passing railroad train ignited the wooden buildings. Rosenthal traveled next to Evansville, Indiana, where he supervised construction of a new plant, after which he was employed by the Crystal Glass Company in Bridgeport, Ohio. He was at Crystal when the Fentons decided to locate in Williamstown, and after the Bastow business erupted, Frank Fenton asked him to go to Williamstown and take over supervision of construction.

In the hot metal department the primary problem was obtaining skilled workers — pressers and finishers—in particular. Unskilled help could be recruited locally, but obviously skilled men could not be found in Williamstown or Marietta, since there were no glass companies in the area. Glass workers, however, were wandering souls—"Travelling flints" was a common nickname for them—and there has always been a heavy migration from one factory to another, so the problem was not as serious, as it might first have appeared. The passing references already made to the numerous plants in which Bastow, Jake Rosenthal, and Frank L. Fenton worked, suggests the high degree of occupational mobility which existed. The word quickly spread when a new plant opened and many of the travelling flints were ready to leave at once. New companies, as well as old, frequently had agents on the road secretly attempting to induce skilled workers to abandon their present employment and go with them.

From scattered FAGCO records and reminiscences of a few old-timers we can piece together a rough account of who worked at the factory in those early days and how they got there. The Jefferson Company in Steubenville provided a number of recruits for FAGCO. Twenty-year old Peter Raymond, for example, received his skilled glassworker's card at Jefferson in 1906. He arrived in Williamstown during the Christmas holidays in 1906, and worked the first day the company was in operation. Raymond remained with Fenton until 1913, when he left, to return in 1921. He retired in 1964 after a glass working career of about 55 years. In his 49 years at FAGCO, Raymond served as presser, finisher, "ringer," and "handler."

Why did Raymond come to Fentons? He came because Bert Coss, for whom he had gathered at Jefferson, had already gone to Williamstown, and Coss wanted him to work as his gatherer there. Why did Coss go to Williamstown? Charles Brand recruited Coss and Fred Herlinger, another "charter worker" at the Williamstown plant, when he visited the Jefferson works in 1906. In the Bastow Case Packet there is a

letter from Coss and Herlinger to Bastow, dated September 30, in which they mention Brand's visit, and ask Bastow if he could find jobs for them at once during construction. Apparently a number of Jefferson people did come down to help in the ground-breaking and construction of the furnace. Coss and Herlinger were among those present on January 2, 1907, when operations began. Coss left for the Heisey glass plant in Newark, Ohio, taking Raymond with him, and never returned. But Herlinger remained at FAGCO until his retirement. He worked principally as a finisher, handler, and occasionally, as a blower.

During the March, 1907 flood, Paul Rosenthal, son of Jake and another of the Jefferson workers, went down to Williamstown, taking Baird Robinson and a few more Jefferson people with him. Prior to this time he had pursued such occupations as farming and barbering, but one day his father asked him if he wanted to learn the glass trade, and he replied he would. Paul caught on quickly and from that time on he usually accompanied his father on his peregrinations. He was, for example, at Greentown in 1903 when the Indiana Tumbler and Goblet Company burned down. In fact, he was near the office when he noticed the fire, and managed to salvage a few records and papers before the intense heat forced him outside. Paul would remain with FAGCO the rest of his career, succeeding his father as factory manager in 1929, and remaining in that capacity until his own retirement 20 years later in 1949.

The earliest "shop" data available is for the first two weeks of November 1907.[6] At that time there were nine shops steadily employed and two others on a part-time schedule. Five of the regular shops were making tumblers, two vases, one goblets, and one

Jacob Rosenthal (front left) and family, sons (l. to r.) Paul, Harry and Clarence and wife Susan.

jug. The composition of the nine shops was as follows with wages per turn (glassworkers work two four and one-half hour "turns" per day) in brackets:

1. Jack Easton ($2.33), G. Green ($2.28), G. Wheatley ($1.45);
2. J. Sullivan ($2.18), Jack Burt ($1.97), Pete Raymond ($1.47);
3. G. Patterson ($2.43), G. Daner ($2.07), W. Keeley ($1.55);
4. J. Gordon ($2.67), C. Terrell ($2.12), W. Gordon ($2.12), J. Jarrett ($1.56);
5. Paul Rosenthal ($2.35), Charles Brand ($2.50), A. Stewart ($2.25), F. Herlinger ($2.25), C. Chalfant ($1.25);
6. Baird Robinson ($2.48), Jimmy Coen ($2.25), Frank Worster ($1.52);
7. C. McCracken ($2.46), H. McCracken ($2.15), C. Miller ($1.49);
8. C. Welch ($1.97), J. O'Donnell ($1.66), Freeman Worster ($1.24);
9. Bert Coss ($2.35), T. R. Smith ($2.75), F. Crum ($1.25).

Molds, of course, play a very critical role in any glass factory. The variety and uniqueness of a line of goods is directly related to the variety and uniqueness of the molds.

In charge of the mold shop from the first days in Williamstown was another Rosenthal, named Clarence, who was the son of Jake and brother of Paul. Assisting Clarence was Frank Smith, plus a work force numbering about six, according to John Noe, and about 12, according to Frank Worster. New designs were scratched in outline on blank molds by Frank L. Fenton, and then Smith and the others would chisel the design into the inside of the mold. It was hard, exacting work, requiring patience and skill. In addition to Clarence Rosenthal and Frank Smith in the mold shop, were Harry Brooks, a lathe operator, a man named Stribble, John Noe, who cleaned the molds, and later, Lem Lewis, who assisted Noe as a mold-cleaner.[7]

Pay for office help was below that for the factory personnel listed above. Grace Sayre, too shy to inquire what her wages would be, was happy to receive $5.00 a week, and overjoyed to have that amount increased by $2.00 within two months' time. John Fenton, company president, received $100 per month in 1907, Charles H., head of the decorating department, $100 per month, and Frank L., secretary-treasurer and general manager, $150 per month.

Pay day was every other Saturday morning, and in cash. After Grace Sayre had become familiar with her duties, she and Robert C. Fenton, another brother who had joined the firm in 1910, would go over to the

[6]*Ironically, it was about this time, on October 24, 1907, that the first reference to what is now known as "carnival" glass turned up in a trade magazine, stating "A new iridescent glass called "Iridill", which has a metallic lustre much like the Tiffany favrile glass, has recently been placed on display. It was made by Fenton . . . and is reasonably priced." On December 5, 1907 another journal extolled "a new line from the Fenton Art Glass Company, which they call 'Iridil'. It . . . is utilized in gas and electric shades, vases and fancy articles. The colorings are very good and the prismatic effects brilliant." A January 9, 1908 report on the Pittsburgh glass exhibit at the Fort Pitt Hotel, with Frank Fenton himself in charge, revealed that their "Iridie" glass was their most recent creation. It was being shown then in a varied line of vases, comports and rose*

bowls. *Perhaps this was just prior to a full-scale immersion into production of table sets and water sets.*
[7]*Without doubt, many of Fenton's early molds were made by the Hipkins Novelty Mould Works of Martins Ferry. Copies of the original mold drawings of the Waterlily and Cattails pattern still exist in the Fenton archives, as well as a bill for molds totalling $5,000. It is also noteworthy to mention here that a mold shop did not exist at Fenton from the very beginning. Two weeks after the company produced it's first piece of glass, it was reported in a January 19, 1907 "China, Glass & Lamps" that FAGCO "decided to install a moldmaking department" and that a factory addition was already under construction.*

Fenton employees, circa 1927 — note Jacob Rosenthal at bottom left.

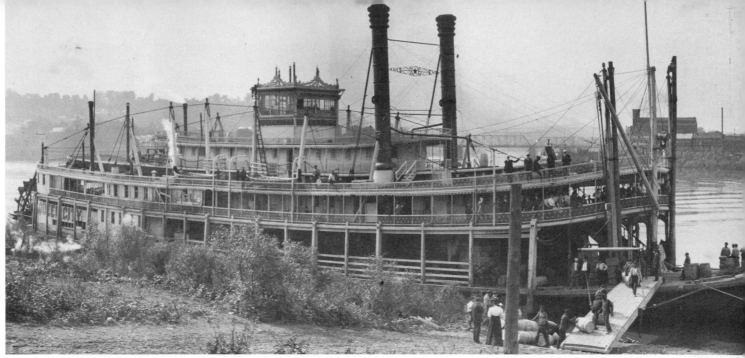

Reportedly this is barrels of glass being loaded onto the Queen City riverboat, in 1907, with buildings from Marietta, Ohio visible in the distance.

First National Bank in Marietta, where FAGCO money was deposited, each Friday afternoon. They had a list of the wages every employee was to receive and went to work filling pay envelopes with the exact amount of cash. The filled envelopes were then stored in the bank vault overnight Friday, and early Saturday morning Robert C.—"one of the few people in the area who owned an automobile"—and Miss Sayre would return to the bank once more, collect the envelopes, and bring them to the factory office. At 11 A.M. on Saturday morning, the employees reported to the office and picked up their pay.

The first few years in Williamstown were characterized by financial ups and downs. Months of profit would be followed by months of declining sales. Many times the Fenton brothers had serious doubts about meeting the Saturday payroll. Frank L. often told his son, Frank M., of those difficult days, when brothers would be sent out in all directions early in the week to scrape up the funds for the weekly payroll. He was not quite sure how they did it, but they never failed to meet a payroll. Thomas Butcher attributed their success in this respect to some mystical quality called "Fenton Luck."

And even though they had a sizeable backlog of orders when the plant opened in January 1907, within two months the company was compelled to negotiate a loan. At a special stockholders meeting March 12, 1907, the directors were authorized to borrow $25,000, but the *Minutes* do not reveal if the company was successful in obtaining this amount of money. Five thousand dollars was loaned FAGCO by the Byesville Foundry, and the First National Bank in Marietta was good for another $4,000. In connection with this latter transaction Frank L. recalled that he ran into the bank president in the street one day when the loan was due. "When are you going to repay the loan, Frank?" queried the president.

"Why anytime you would like it," replied Fenton. "Would you like it now?"

"Oh, no," was the rejoinder. "I was just curious." The bluff worked—for the loan could not possibly have been repaid then — and the money was not demanded.

All FAGCO products, in those first years, were shipped out in wooden barrels. A cooperage shop was located opposite the shipping room on the West side of the railroad spur. and in the shop, three men were kept busy making barrels. The hoops and staves were purchased. but the coopers put the barrels together. The barrels were then carried right through an open box-car which was usually stationed at that point on the track, into the shipping room. Ray Umpleby gave the packers, one of whom was Ernie Metcalfe, the packing orders, and the barrels would then be filled with glassware. carefully packed in straw. When they were ready to go, Bedilion. the shipping clerk, would take them out on the platform and stencil or write the address of their ultimate destination on the barrels. Box-cars. loaded with barrels, would be run down to the Williamstown Baltimore and Ohio Railroad depot at regular intervals, where they would eventually be coupled to freight trains for the trip to market.

In the beginning the company's major sales representative was George Mortimer of New York. Mortimer, who was the agent for other glass companies besides FAGCO, had many contacts with retail chain stores, such as Woolworth's. Kresge's, McCrory's, and Kress. It was through this type of outlet and large wholesale outlets like Butler Brothers (see page 115) that much Fenton ware was marketed. Most of the business was in the East and Midwest, although the company occasionally received substantial orders from the Far West. In later years, other sales representatives were added until the entire country was blanketed.[8]

[8]*In December, 1908, the following note appeared in "Glass & Pottery World", concerning Fenton's new carnival glass, "The iridescent glass put out by (FAGCO) and known to the manufacturers as "Rubi glass" has been enjoying a great sale, especially in the ten cent stores. H. Northwood & Co. have just produced a line almost identical in color with the Fenton output. It will be called 'Golden Iris'." The story went on to editorialize, "It seems a pity that a glass so much like the Tiffany "Favrile" product, save in weight, should find the counters of the cheap stores. However, these are days when a heavy bulk production is necessary to make even a light profit, and sentiment rarely outweighs dollars when pay rolls are to be considered."*

III
SOME READJUSTMENTS

The first three or four years in Williamstown were marked by the moderate shuffling of official personnel. Principally, this involved the departure of one Fenton brother and the arrival of two others, for a net gain of one. The exiting brother was John, who with Frank had founded the company, who had been the central figure in the transfer to Williamstown, and who had taken over the presidency when Dent resigned late in 1907. The circumstances attending John's leaving have been so shrouded in mystery for over half a century that it has become impossible to unveil the true story. Although every person who was interviewed in connection with FAGCO's early history was asked ritualistically, "Why did John leave?" none knew for sure and could only speculate.

We do know that the two men were totally unalike in temperament and personality and that some kind of break was inevitable. Family relations and friends who knew John and Frank best agree that both were given to command, and that the time had to come when one of them, probably John, would no longer tolerate the other. John became president in 1907 while Frank remained general manager, yet the latter was paid more than the former. This was an unusual situation in itself, but there was much more to the dispute. John has been characterized as an "operator," or a "promoter," a person with big ideas and lots of ambition, but little perseverance. He was good at initiating a project, but poor at finishing one. Frank, on the other hand, who was conservative by nature and dedicated to long-range company stability, must have found John's flightiness appalling.

One incident which illustrates John's impetuosity and which no doubt contributed to the split, was told to Frank M. Fenton by his father and Uncle Charles. A large order had been received by the company. The following day when Charles reported for work he found a truck dumping sand and gravel outside the factory. "What's this for?" he inquired of John, who was supervising the unloading.

"Why," came the reply, "we got that big order yesterday, so we're going to build another furnace."

Charles went to Frank with the story and insisted that another furnace was not only unnecessary, but also financially unfeasible at that time. Frank agreed with him and the furnace was not built.

In a somewhat similar vein, Lem Lewis recalls the time when John, without telling anyone, paid out $800 for a large lathe. Beeson chided him, saying, "You don't need that at all."

"You never can tell," was the confident response. But that was John's impulsive way; grand action with little thought of the consequences.

John was bright and enterprising; he knew how to make money, but not how to keep it. "If he got $1,000 in the bankbook he'd go wild," remarked Lewis. A friend who admired John very much once said, "he could talk your pockets inside out." John was always going to make a million dollars. And even when he did not have a dime, which was not infrequently, he acted as if he had a million dollars. Sometime in the fall of 1909 John left Williamstown for Millersburg, Ohio, and within the next few months he had sold his interest in the Fenton company. In Millersburg, typically he opened a new glass plant which shut down in a short time, reopened and then shut down for good.

The two brothers who joined the company during these years of transition were James E., and Robert C. James was born in 1870 in Homer City, Pennsylvania, a few miles south of Indiana. He learned the plumbing and tinning trades in Indiana and for many years was employed in those capacities by a Mr. Taylor. In 1908, after the Williamstown plant opened, John Fenton made two trips back to the family home in an effort to induce James to join FAGCO. Following the first trip, Taylor offered James more money so he decided to remain in Indiana. But the second mission was successful because before Christmas 1908 James was in Williamstown working as maintenance supervisor for the company.

This could not have been an easy decision for him to make. For one thing, the offer of an attractive business was dropped in James' lap in Indiana just as he was about to leave. His associate-to-be told him, "Jim, if you stay here you can name your own price." But he decided to go and the associate-to-be who stayed prospered mightily in his new enterprise. Another disturbing factor for James was that his wife, the former Nettie Clawson, whom he had married in the 1890's, was seriously ill with cancer in a Pittsburgh hospital. James came to Williamstown by himself in 1908, with the family following in the spring of 1909. His wife was placed in a Marietta hospital immediately upon her arrival, was operated upon and lived for only seven weeks. In 1910 James married Mrs. Flora Legleitner Sprague. Four children were born to each of the two unions.

Robert C. Fenton, the oldest of the six brothers, was born in Indiana, Pennsylvania, in 1868, but was the last of them to join FAGCO. At the age of 17 he left home and went to stay with relatives in Mansfield, Ohio. Very shortly he moved on to Marion, where he settled down and would live for the next 25 years. During that time he served as dispatcher and telegraph operator for the Erie Railroad Company's relay office in Marion. In 1890 he married Grace E. Dudley, and all three children, two boys and a girl, were born in Marion.

When John Fenton founded the Millersburg glass plant in 1909, he talked Robert into coming to work for him.[9] Robert thereupon secured a leave of absence from the railroad and went to Millersburg for a brief period. He did return to Marion, but the glass business must have appealed to him, because in the latter part of 1910 he came to Williamstown and would soon be the number two man in the FAGCO hierarchy. The record does not reveal what overtures were made by Frank to bring Robert to Williamstown, but no doubt some were made. As with James, Robert did not bring his family down until he was well-established, which was in the fall of 1911. Although Robert never held an official position with FAGCO until he became secretary in 1925, he owned stock as early as 1908, and took charge of sales operations almost as soon as he joined the company. His daughter, Mrs. Ethel Queen, remembers his frequent departures on two or three week trips with a suitcase full of glassware.

Reorganization of the company in 1910 found Frank Fenton now assuming the presidency in addition to his jobs as treasurer and general manager. He did turn over the secretaryship to Howells, while Beeson, who had become vice-president in 1907, retained that post. Early in 1911 Charles H. Fenton, who had been foreman of the Decorating Department since the plant opened in Williamstown, was elected assistant general manager and second vice-president. This four-man lineup remained unchanged, with two exceptions, for over 20 years. Those exceptions took place in 1925 when Robert C. Fenton supplanted Howells as secretary, and in 1926 when Howells replaced Charles as second vice-president. Several changes occurred in the 1930's with the deaths of Beeson in 1931 and Charles in 1936, and the retirement of Howells from the Board in 1934. By the end of that decade the two principal officers in the company were Frank, who was still president, treasurer, and general manager, and Robert, who was vice-president, secretary, and sales manager.

The other brother, Charles, who suffered a leg injury as a boy in a train accident, always stayed close to Frank. Mrs. Frank L. Fenton often heard the story that her husband never took a job anywhere without making sure that there was a place for Charles. Consequently, when he established his own company, he put Charles on the payroll at once and he remained there until his death in 1936. In 1907, while his salary was $100 per month, he was given a $3,000 bonus or 30 shares of stock to be pro rated over the next five years, a further indication of Frank's interest in his brother's welfare and security.

One further family adjustment, although not of a business nature, was the marriage of Frank L. Fenton to Lillian Muhleman of Bridgeport, Ohio, on June 26, 1907. They had first met while Frank was either working for Northwood in Wheeling, or after he had launched his own decorating plant in Martins Ferry. When the company was reorganized in Williamstown in the winter of 1906-07, Lillian was employed as a teller and secretary at the Security Trust Company in Wheeling. It was while she was there, in March 1907, that FAGCO negotiated a fairly sizeable loan from Security Trust.

Construction of a new home at 409 Williams Avenue was begun at once, and late in 1908 they moved into that structure. The family grew fast, however, six daughters and two sons within 15 years, and soon the Williams Avenue home no longer sufficed. After the birth of the eighth and last child, Wilmer C., in 1923, it was decided to purchase the Charles Dowling house at 410 Fourth Street overlooking the Ohio River. This large building was completely remodeled inside and out and was ready for occupancy in 1924. For most of the Fenton children this was the home of their childhood, and as Frank M. has said, "it was fun to grow up there."

*　　*　　*　　*

The question of joining the National Association of Manufacturers of Pressed and Blown Glassware (hereafter called the "Association"), national trade organization for the industry with headquarters in Pittsburgh, was first raised in the fall of 1907. John Kunzler, secretary for the body, apparently wrote FAGCO and invited it to join the Association, but at a November 5 stockholders meeting, action on the proposal was deferred until the January meeting. At that time the stockholders voted to let the decision rest with the Directors. For some reason the Directors let the matter slide because on March 18, 1909, over a year later, Kunzler again wrote the company. "Thinking perhaps you may have forgotten this matter," he said, "we again invite you to join this Association and become a member thereof. This Association is a necessity and every employer of the members of the American Flint Glassworkers Union should be a member thereof." The offer was accepted this time, as letters of May 6 and 20 from Kunzler reported that "you have been elected to membership in this Association."

Services provided by the Association were financed by quarterly assessments on all member companies at $1.00 per pot. These services consisted of providing information on wage lists, moves, wages, rules,

---

[9]*The possibilities of FAGCO involvement in the Millersburg concern are even more intriguing by this quote which appeared in a June 1909 "Pottery & Glass". It stated that the Millersburg Glass Company was organized chiefly with "capital from Marietta, O., and Williamstown, W. Va." A year earlier, in a July, 1908 issue of "China, Glass & Lamps" a brief item claimed that "Millersburg, O. is trying to land a new factory. (FAGCO) is looking for a location. They want about three acres near a railroad and a concrete block building 150 feet in length and proportionately wide. They expect to employ 125 boys and possibly 75 girls."*

It is possible, indeed likely, that these notices were written and submitted to the trade journals by John Fenton personally. He was quite a promoter and perhaps entered the Millersburg venture without full compliance from his brothers. At some point John must have

been disillusioned with his Williamstown ties. A February 11, 1909 "China, Glass and Lamps" report, complete with pictures of the Millersburg factory stated, "The business is under the direct control of J. W. Fenton. However, there are no business relations whatever between the Williamstown and Millersburg factory directly or indirectly."

There are no records connecting any actual company involvement between FAGCO and Millersburg. However, Frank M. Fenton recalls his Uncle Robert saying "The Millersburg plant kept going all right until we cut the pipeline sending milk up there". Perhaps the involvement was strictly on a personal family level, which would explain why the company Minutes include no mention of Millersburg or John Fenton, after 1910.

and other agreements dealing with labor-management relations. All skilled glassworkers belonged to the American Flint Glassworkers Union (hereafter referred to as the AFGWU), and whenever local wage agreements were to be negotiated the union's demands and the company's proposals would be largely governed by prevailing national standards. The Association was able to supply this information. For example, in Kunzler's May 20 letter to FAGCO, he included a copy of a recent agreement worked out between the Association and the AFGWU for the manufacture of "solid stem comports." The item itself is first described, with the exact dimensions set forth, after which the pay rates for the various jobs are listed. For the four-inch article there should be a 775 move (the number of items produced in one four and one-half hour turn), for which the presser should receive $2.00, the finisher $1.75, and the gatherer $1.25. But for the ten-inch comport there should be only a 280 move, with the presser receiving $2.50, the finisher $2.00, and the gatherer $1.70. Consequently, the Association was a clearing-house of necessary information for all producers and it was wise to belong. However, in 1951, by which time the machine glass manufacturers had won control of the Association from the hand glass plants, FAGCO withdrew.

Turning to labor affairs, the AFGWU was organized in 1878, and embraced all skilled workers—gatherers, pressers, and finishers—in hand-operated glass plants in both the United States and Canada. A new company, like FAGCO in 1907, necessarily must have a local branch of the AFGWU right from the beginning because it had to hire gatherers, pressers, and finishers, all of whom were union members. About a month after operations began in Williamstown, the national AFGWU headquarters in Toledo sent a representative to FAGCO and the local union, Number 22, was formally organized. According to "Pete" Raymond's recollection, George Green, a finisher, was the first man to chairman the local's executive committee, which would conduct all the union's negotiations with the company.

Raymond also recalls an amusing incident of those early days when the local was trying to beef up its treasury. "You know, we had no money at all," he reminded his interviewer. Union meetings were held in a room above a saloon on Front Street, and most of the sessions were devoted to fund-raising ideas. A number of proposals were advanced, but none seemed acceptable until someone suggested a dance. The only musical accompaniment would be on a drum and a piano, but they felt that by charging 50 cents a person they could make some money. At length one chap, well aware of the reputation some glassworkers had for not being the most stable citizens in a community, roared out, "Mr. Chairman, we'd better do this quick before we are found out."

Labor-management relations at FAGCO were very good right from the outset of operations and have remained so. The hand glass industry, where workers possess rare skills and have an impassioned pride in their product, apparently lends itself to greater labor stability than most modern industrial trades. All disputes and agreements between the workers and company officials were handled by the union committee, which usually numbered from three to five men. The committee chairman was elected by the full union membership on an annual basis. If the chairman proved an able one he would often be elected and reelected over a period of years. The chairman personally selected his own committee.

The machinery for adjusting labor-management disputes in the glass-making field was far more sophisticated than in most other enterprises. Wildcat strikes, sit-down strikes, lockouts, boycotts, labor spies, Pinkerton detectives, violence and death, all characteristic of heavy industrial capitalism during the "Gilded Age" and beyond, were unknown in the glass-making business. Peaceful mediation of disputes was the practice here long before it was used in most other fields. The agreements for pay scales for the different jobs were worked out at regular negotiating sessions between the Association and the AFGWU.

Grievances against the company were adjusted by the following procedure: The first step was the filing of a formal "Protest," containing the substance of the complaint, and the protest would be signed by the union committee and a company representative. No strike, lockout, or walkout occurred; work was simply carried on as usual while the protest was being formally processed. Usually during the annual contract talks, a special meeting of representatives from both management and the AFGWU was held, at which all the accumulated protests were discussed and settled. If a protest was resolved in favor of the worker, the company would have to give him his back pay or whatever emoluments he had coming to him. If it was decided in favor of the company, the grievance was denied. All findings were binding on both sides, and rarely have they ever been challenged. "Doc" Bennett, who was active in union affairs for over 50 years, both at FAGCO and elsewhere, remembers only one national strike in all that time.

Glassworkers were carefree, happy souls in those relatively uncomplicated days before World War I. They would move from job to job with the unworried indifference of youth, always looking for "greener fields." During the long summer shutdowns they would loaf and camp together, sometimes just the men themselves, and at other times, with reduced conviviality, entire families were included. "Pete" Raymond has vivid memories—aided by some telltale photographs—of such a camp in 1908 located near the point where Duck Creek enters the Ohio River. The camp was actually controlled by some glassworkers from Cumberland, Maryland, but they graciously welcomed all fellow craftsmen and many FAGCO people accepted their invitation.

The unstated penchant to move around in search of a better situation—the "traveling flint" complex—can be well illustrated by a brief look at the careers of two FAGCO veterans, "Doc" Bennett and Raymond, who plied their trade collectively for well over 100 years. Bennett learned glass-making at the Beaumont plant in Grafton, West Virginia, in 1902, and when Beaumont closed down in 1909 he moved up to Millersburg in John Fenton's new factory. When the latter plant closed he went over to Fairmont, West Virginia, and in 1911 joined FAGCO. He stayed in Williamstown only 14 weeks at this time, however, for when John Fenton got things running again in Millersburg,

Bennett returned there. Millersburg closed for good in 1913, after which Bennett worked in several places, winding up at a glass house in New Martinsville, West Virginia in the early 1920's. In 1923 he learned of a presser vacancy at FAGCO, and after writing a letter of inquiry, was offered the job by Jake Rosenthal. He accepted it and remained at Fentons until his retirement in June 1955.

Raymond actually began his career at the age of nine as a carrying-over boy in Leasureville, West Virginia, but he did not receive his skilled worker's card until he completed his apprenticeship at Steubenville's Jefferson plant in 1906. As was noted earlier, he came to FAGCO when it opened its doors in Williamstown in January 1907, and stayed there until 1913, when his wanderings began. He went first to Heisey's in Newark, then in 1916 to Jeannette, Pennsylvania, and then back to Newark. In the war years he turned to boilermaking, got a union card, and worked in the railroads at Newark. With the war over and the economy slowing down, Raymond was furloughed for several months, but finally caught on again at

FAGCO in 1921. When he left Fentons in 1913, he was advised by Jake Rosenthal of the folly of job-changing—"new fields look good, till after you get into them." Jake did add, however, that "if things don't pan out the way you think they will, and if I have a place, you'll get it." In 1921 Rosenthal had a place for Raymond, so back he came.

Occasionally the *Minutes* carry reports of current business affairs made by Frank L. Fenton in his capacity as president and general manager. In November 1907, for example, he stated that earnings for the first ten months of the year totalled $15,000, that plenty of orders were on hand, and that future prospects were bright. The October 1910 report on the previous months and the outlook of things to come was "quite satisfactory." Two months later "the outlook for business was good, as orders were being placed for next year's business." In November 1912 the general manager's oral report shows that "the business is going along as favorably as we could wish."[10]

IV
GROWTH AND AFFLUENCE

With the Williamstown plant on a firm foundation and in the hands of responsible leaders, FAGCO now entered a period of lengthy prosperity which was interrupted only by the Great Depression. In the years from 1910 to 1930 sales rose steadily and dividends and bonuses were declared with great frequency. Salary increases for the officers and stock increases for the shareholders were made periodically, as the company moved on to its most affluent years in the early 1920's. World War I, it is true, caused a labor shortage, but workers were obtained, and plant operations slowed down only briefly. While the records are not absolutely complete for these years, we still have enough to draw a reasonably accurate picture of FAGCO's expanding operations in the two decades before the depression.

In surveying the financial history of the Fenton Company from 1910-30, we find a prosperous beginning, a wartime slow-down, a sharp pickup after the war, a tremendous boom in the mid-twenties, and a rather steady decline in the late twenties as the depression began to set in. Prior to 1927 the only annual deficit recorded was in 1914, when World War I erupted.[11] It so happens that the one "annual report" to be found in the company Archives for the pre-depression years was for 1914, and it clearly sets forth some of the problems plaguing the company at that time. Because it is brief and because any attempt to summarize it would drain it of its flavor, the report is reproduced here in full.

"The year 1914 started out fine. Shipments for January and February being fully equal to

shipments in the same months of our biggest years. March ushered in a general slump in business that extended over the entire country and showed itself in our business by a falling off in shipments of $7,000 over the previous month. Conditions seemed to improve in April, May, and June and led us to believe that with a good fall business, we should show a nice gain at the end of the year, but the European War hit us in the middle of the year and the country has not yet recovered the shock. Added to this, our shipping was hampered by the prevalence of the Hoof and Mouth disease and at times, almost closed the plant down. Packing material was at a premium and we were compelled to pay as high as $19 per ton for this material.

"These remarks preface our general statement which shows that in spite of conditions, we have paid the dividends on preferred stock, maintained the value on our common stock and kept the plant in first class running condition. We do not know what the year 1915 will bring us but we are hoping for a good big year. Our new designs and decorations are better than those of previous years and with good general conditions, we believe that money will be made and prosperity will be with us.

"The directors of the company have felt that in view of general conditions that we carry out a policy of retrenchment that would affect every part of the plant. In accordance with this policy, a general reduction of 15% in salaries

[10]*In October, 1912, a report in the "trade notes" section of the "Flint" (the official publication of the American Flint Glass Workers Union) stated, "(FAGCO) is doing an exceedingly large amount of business on a general line of blown and pressed wares. The company has recently started in the light cutting business and is increasing its capacity nearly every week. It practically owns Williamstown, which is growing very rapidly." In this same periodical in April, 1914, the expansion of this cutting department was announced."*

[11]*On April 14, 1914, "The Pottery Gazette", an English trade journal, proclaimed "The Fenton . . . wares are freely represented. They have been responsible for a new rose tinted glass having an amber edge, which is supplied in dishes, plates, nappies, vases and bon-bons. This is an advance line of a quite new production which is being brought out to replace, or at least to assist, the iridescent glassware, of which a great quantity is sold in the North of England and by the bazaars." I am not certain to what they are referring, unless it is some form of amberina iridescent glass.*

has taken effect including all salaried employees drawing a salary of $100 per month or over . . . "

Following World War I, business improved with each year, reaching a peak in 1922. For the period from 1917 to 1925, the most consistently profitable stretch until World War II, profits averaged 9% of sales. They held firm at 8% until the banner year of 1922, when they zoomed to 15%, after which they dropped back to 8%. Signs of trouble were apparent in the profit-loss picture for 1926, and in the following two years the company lost money. FAGCO made a good recovery in 1929, but 1930 marked the beginning of a long and difficult decade, which will be described in the next book. Fenton's "net worth" (capital plus surplus) naturally grew steadily in the post-World War I years, reflecting improved business conditions. Lagging slightly behind the profits growth, the net worth peak was reached in 1925 at $273,000. In the ensuing years it dropped regularly as the impact of the depression became more pronounced.

At no time in FAGCO history was the manpower shortage as acute as it was during World War I. The rewards for employment in defense and war plants were apparently so much greater than those in a glass factory, that Fentons had to send recruiting agents into the country. The best-remembered instance of this was in July 1916 when Beeson and James Fenton travelled to Millwood, West Virginia, a small river town about 45 miles southwest of Parkersburg, in search of help. Other communities may have also been explored at this time, but the Millwood operation was most successful because no less than 32 men and boys, mostly boys, were enlisted for service with FAGCO.

The whole crowd, teen-age boys for the most part, travelled to the Marietta suburb by train within the next few days. Not all of them stayed at FAGCO once they got there, yet many did and Snyder and Badgley would spend the rest of their lives in Williamstown. But where to house all these young people once they arrived in town? After all, they were but boys, and in the case of Badgley, his mother did not know, at least for a week, that he had even left Millwood. Well, arrangements were made with a Mrs. Ullman, who owned a two-story house on Second Street a block or so west of Highland Avenue, to provide room and board for most of the newcomers. The boys themselves were to pay the first $2.50 of their weekly expenses, but above that the company picked up the bill. Food, lodging, laundry, all the necessaries, were taken care of in this fashion. A cook and waitress were even hired to handle the heavy traffic. Mrs. Ullman packed lunches for everyone, which they carried to the factory in little black tin buckets. Badgley recalls that you could see the empty buckets scattered all the way between Ullman's and Fentons, as the boys would ungraciously cast them aside after consuming the contents.

To handle the overflow of neophyte glass-workers a big tent was set up in Ullman's backyard, which held from ten to twelve cots. Obviously, throwing a pack of spirited boys together in dormitory fashion— "we all moved to Mrs. Ullman's like a bunch of rubes" —was not conducive to orderly housekeeping, and

rough-houses became nightly affairs. "It was nothing," says Badgley, "to see the feathers flying out of there when they got in a pillow fight." Some of the group was also domiciled in rooms above a restaurant on Highland at the railroad tracks, while others were scattered about town in private homes. Mrs. Ullman's health was not good, and it became necessary to break up the "Fenton Hotel" within a year or so. Gradually the boys who stayed on became young men and established their own homesteads.

The labor shortage was so pressing in World War I that for the first time in its history FAGCO hired female employees to work in the hot metal department.[12] The factory of a glass plant is not the most pleasant place in which to work, chiefly because of the heat, and it must not have been an easy choice to decide to hire women. As Henry Snyder said, "I wouldn't want any daughter of mine working out there." At any rate, on Monday morning, September 24, 1917, the first women factory employees reported for duty. A notice posted in the plant announced that " . . . we trust that each man and boy will be as kind and courteous to them as you would be to your own mother or sister. They are coming here to earn their living the same as you are and we want you to help them make good." No one knows how many females were brought in to the factory in those war years, but not many of them lasted long. Two, however, Mrs. Alice Brookover and Mrs. Toots Flowers—Alice and "Toots," as they were called—stayed on and were still working at FAGCO in World War II.

One of Snyder's two most vivid memories was the celebration at the news of the armistice ending World War I. Word of an armistice was received on November 7, 1918—the famous Roy Howard "scoop"— but this was proven false before anyone at FAGCO had time to organize a celebration. Then when the official report came in four days later, long metal sheets were ripped down from the glory-holes and everyone in the factory began shouting wildly and jumping up and down on the metal strips. "You never heard such a racket." Having exhausted themselves in this fashion, the entire force then left, and the plant, like nearly all other business establishments, simply closed down.

The supply of natural gas was in jeopardy occasionally during World War I, because of industrial needs and some very cold winters. A few FAGCO old-timers vaguely recall that the federal government might have arbitrarily cut off gas for non-essential industry, but this probably was not done. Frank Worster does assert, however, that early in 1917, when the temperature remained below zero for some time, the gas was cut down for several weeks, so that it was impossible to operate the factory although the pots were kept warm. Lawrence Badgley also recalls

---

[12]On June 28, 1917, "The Pottery, Brass & Glass Salesman" made the first known reference to Fenton's "Stretch" glass. "From Fenton . . . a beautiful line of iridescent glassware. Included in the showing are novel baskets with handformed handles in a dainty silvery iridescence. The line has been correctly named "Silver Sun" and is shown in a number of iridescent colorings. Every piece is in a different shade, while some have been produced in a striking crackled effect.

that several other cold snaps during the war compelled temporary shutdowns.[13]

The problem of gas remained after the war too, because at the Board of Directors meeting on December 2, 1919, much of the time was devoted to discussing a recent rate increase instituted by the Hope Natural Gas Company, FAGCO's principal supplier. The general manager was instructed to negotiate the best possible agreement with the Hope people, but nothing is reported on the outcome of these talks if they ever occurred. However, a few months later a five year lease was granted to FAGCO on 40 acres of potential gas and oil property in the Williams District of Wood County by one Fred Delancy. Fenton had to drill a well within three months or forfeit the lease. If gas or oil was found, the Delancys were entitled to either a small percentage of the output or a flat $150 annual fee. But again there is no evidence that anything significant emerged from this arrangement.

Two new employees, hired in the middle 1920's and who would spend nearly forty years each with FAGCO, were Francis Lehew and Bernard "Butch" Malone. Lehew, who was born and raised in Paden City, West Virginia, got his union card as a moldmaker in 1921, and worked in several different glass plants in the next few years. During the winter of 1923-24 he was at the Davis Glass Company in Martins-Ferry, but that factory closed in April 1924, leaving everyone who was employed there without a job. Back in Paden City Lehew noticed in the industry's trade journal that the Fenton Company needed a moldmaker for three months, so he caught the first train to Williamstown, had an interview with mold shop foreman Clarence Rosenthal, and got the job. He went to work on April 24, renting a room in the Dowling house on 4th Street, on the property Frank L. Fenton would shortly acquire for his own family. And just when the three-month assignment was completed, Earl Wildermuth, a lathe man in the mold shop, decided to change jobs and went over to Marietta Concrete. Lehew fell right into this vacancy.

Late in 1926, by which time Lehew was chairman of the union committee, a minor wage dispute broke out between the union and the company. As spokesman for the committee, he kept pressing Frank L. to grant the workers an increase, but the president kept putting him off. After several weeks of this, Frank finally told Lehew that he was going to give everyone a 10 cent an hour increase except the committee chairman. "I pestered him so much that I guess he was getting back at me," Lehew reflected. Irked at this development, Lehew quit his job and went to Corning, New York, hoping to catch on with the glass company there. He did not get a job at Corning, however, and returned to Williamstown. Too proud to ask for his job back, he and his wife opened a little confectioner's stand at Putnam and Seventh Street in Marietta. In July or August of 1927, one of the mold workers quit

at FAGCO and Clarence Rosenthal came to Lehew and asked him if he would like to go back to work on a temporary basis. Altho Lehew was eager to return to Fentons he was still too proud to appear too eager, so he said he would prefer a permanent position. After further discussion, the company agreed to this and Lehew returned to his former job. He became assistant foreman of the mold shop in 1945 and foreman in 1949, a post he held until his retirement in 1964.

Malone was first employed at FAGCO in 1926. He was 16 at the time and as there had been trouble at home, it was necessary for him to go out and find work. Although he knew the Rosenthals it was not through this connection that he was hired by Fenton. He simply came over to the factory one day, asked Bert Fenton for a job, and got one. Recalling this experience 40 years later, Malone said, "it wasn't like it is now, when you have to take all those tests before you can get a job. Then you just walked in off the street and they put you to work. Later on someone would come around and take your name." Malone worked steadily until the depression put him out of a job, either in 1931 or 1932. In the next seven years or so he did a number of things, like managing his grandparents grocery store and painting houses. For five years he did building construction and road maintenance under WPA. All the while he kept in touch with Paul Rosenthal about conditions at the glass factory and as business began to improve in 1939 he returned there to work. Since that time Malone became a ring and handle gatherer, in addition to serving almost continually as a committeeman for the miscellaneous workers union.

In 1925 FAGCO imported a special four-man shop — two Swedes, a Frenchman and a Czecho-Slovak — to make "offhand" ware.[14] Offhand ware is a special kind of glass product made without molds; it is very beautiful, but requires highly-skilled workmen and is quite costly. After the basic form of the piece is produced by blowing, intricate designs are attached to it manually, and thru a continual reheating process, these designs are gradually worked into the original pattern. The Fenton company hired the "offhand shop" under a one-year contract, with guaranteed wages for each of the four men, whether they worked or not. The shop head was guaranteed the unbelievable pay of $25.00 per day. It was evident, however, long before the one year was over, that offhand ware, despite its beauty, was not moving, so the experiment was abandoned, and the shop was broken up.[15]

Working in a glass factory stimulated the imagination of several workers, who developed new devices to improve production. Violet Ruf recalls that her father, James E. Fenton, once invented a little "gimmick" to be attached to the press and Frank L. was seriously considering applying for a patent on it, when it was discovered that the device had already been

[13]*Apparently, not only the company suffered during the war. A March, 1917, report in the "Flint" reported that workers were at "One-third time", primarily because of gas supply shortages.*

[14]*Two of these men were Oscar Ecksted and Fritz Alberg. The other two were a Mr. Peterson and a Mr. Brandt, first names unknown.*

[15]*Although this does not directly concern the Fenton history, it does concern one of the family's most interesting members, John*

W. Fenton. A December, 1927, issue of American Flint carried a report of the sale of the "old" Northwood plant at Wheeling. It claimed that J. W. Fenton was named as the firm's new general manager. It also stated that "while the Northwood plant is being remodeled into a modern plant, Mr. Fenton is working on new molds and coloring processes for making and decorating their new wares." Apparently this was another failure in John's life, since the Northwood factory never did re-open. I find it small wonder that the man appeared so glum in the family portrait.

The Founding Generation as pictured in 1930; (Back row, l. to r.) Charles H. Fenton, Frank L. Fenton, James E. Fenton, and William H. Fenton, who was not associated with the company; (Front row, l. to r.) John W. Fenton, Gertrude E. Brand (sister) and Robert C. Fenton.

patented. Another inventor was Charles Brand, who had married Frank L's. sister, Gertrude, back in Indiana, Pennsylvania, and who worked as a handler for several years after the Williamstown plant opened. He had an abscessed tooth, which required an operation which, in turn, led to his death early in 1910, but before that, he perfected a spray used to decorate vases and other items. In 1922 FAGCO directors voted to pay Gertrude Brand $50 a month for the rest of her life "in consideration of the services performed by her husband . . . in originating and perfecting the spraying device used by the Company for the past 13 years." Actually, the spraying instrument was not that unique, and it was probably used as an excuse to provide the widowed sister with a regular and needed income.[16]

V
DEPRESSION YEARS

It should surprise no one to learn that the Great Depression was the most critical period in Fenton history. The decline, already begun in the late 1920's, gathered a full head of steam in the next few years, lasting until 1939. From 1931 through 1938 five deficits were recorded, and in the other three years, the margin of gain was so narrow as to be inconsequential. Money was borrowed from every conceivable source, dividend payments were suspended, insurance policies were mortgaged, and wages and salaries were slashed. With orders falling off substantially— although the plant never closed for lack of business— it was necessary to divide up the available work among all employees. In some of the worst moments a man might consider himself fortunate to get six turns a week.

EDITOR'S NOTE:

Here we interrupt Dr. Murdock's history with a preview of the Depression years. We will continue his manuscript in our proposed sequel covering the second twenty-five years of The Fenton Art Glass Company.

[16]*On April 14, 1924, "China, Glass & Lamps" mentions "A new line of Fenton Glass is made in Venetian red in marbled effect. A new note is given by using cobalt bases instead of black, and the combination . . . is much more alive . . . than with black. Another Fenton item that is unusual is a line that includes as yet only ice tea and lemonade sets and vases of striped opaque and clear yellowish green glass, with handles and coasters of cobalt. The color is known as Victoria green."*

On September 22, 1925, this note appeared in a trade journal concerning Fenton's newest lines, "There are several lovely bowls in iridescent topaz, and exquisite shade, shallow floating bowls, cupped bowls with wide flare and a large salad bowl with plate to match. One very good number is a nut set consisting of one footed bowl with six small individual cups. In the same color comes a sweetmeat set divided into four compartments with removable center cup."

On January 18, 1926, "China, Glass & Lamps" offered this report concerning Fenton's new line of art glass and red slag, "From its off-hand shop, where each piece is made of two colors in glass, there are some notable productions. First, there is the 'Karnak Red' which has designs worked in it in black glass. One vase is 22 inches tall. The 'Mosaic' treatment shows little pieces of vari-colored glass set into black glass. In shapes and treatments similar to the 'Karnak Red' are 'Oriental Ivory', 'Antique Green', and 'Turquoise Blue'. A new color in refreshment sets, lemonade sets and vases is 'Victoria Topaz' on a new shape. An unusual red in ebonized effect is the 'Venetian Red' which comes in a variety of smaller pieces including jars, boxes and candlesticks and bowls. Fan vases in four sizes and a selection of nearly 50 colors and decorative treatments make the choice of these quite remarkable."

On January 27, 1927 "The Pottery, Glass & Brass Salesman" extolled that "Particularly striking is, the "Cameo" line. This shows a translucent pinkish opal shade fading into a transparent golden tone. The almost silky appearance of the translucent portion, which invariably is the edge, is strikingly in harmonious contrast with the transparent part which constitutes the body.

'Both the tangerine and the ruby line are self-descriptive. The ruby, incidentally, is cased, and so is the particularly beautiful peach blow, the name of which as well is self-descriptive."

In 1927, the first reports about the Fenton Turtle appeared in trade journals. On June 9, it was stated that Fenton "has recently brought out a novelty in fancy glassware in the form of a turtle. The turtle, which is shown only in green glass, is between 6 and 7 inches in length, and has a hollow center part which could serve as a jewelry or trinket case. It can also be used as a flower bowl by leaving off the top and inserting in the well a smaller turtle flower block, the latter an exact replica in shape of the larger turtle." And then, on October 6, another report announced "Among (Fenton's) latest is an aquarium. The base has been modeled in the form of a turtle in a pretty green color into which is fitted the aquarium which is crystal. The bowl is made of bubble effect glass which gives a pretty appearance when filled with water. The piece complete stands about eight inches high. There are also some brand new bowls with candlesticks to match in various original shapes and a number of different colors, such as rose, amber, green, canary, blue, etc."

On January 16, 1928, "China, Glass & Lamps" mentioned two unusual new items by Fenton. "In art glassware, (Fenton) has two new shapes in plain colors and some very unusual two-color effects. In the latter ware the main color is flecked at the scalloped edge with white. The two combinations are white against ruby and white against a light chocolate. The effects are gained through the working of the colored glass while still hot and offers a distinct novelty."

On February, 1930, another trade journal report noticed "A revival of opalescent glass was noticeable in the display of the Fenton Art Glass Co. This glass, which came into prominance nearly a half-century ago, has had spurts of popularity since then, and Fenton has some attractive new pieces, with both spiral and straight optics. Large opalescent pitchers with black glass handles were shown, and so were iced tea sets in several designs. Ivy bowls made a particularly good showing in the opalescent glass."

The same report went on to state, "Fenton brought out a new lilac color this year, and they had their stemware in this shade on display. Jade urns, Grecian both in shape and decorations, with lights shining through, occupied a place of honor in the Fenton showing. More utilitarian were the new and attractive shaped orange reamers and bowls, in jade and black. There was also a line of utility bowls in jade and black, as well as jade salts and peppers in black handled holders."

INDEX

(N.I. — Not Illustrated)

NOTES

NOTES